RISING TO *Feminine* POWER

THE LASSO OF TRUTH

JOSEPHINE PALERMO Ph.D.

First published by Ultimate World Publishing 2023
Copyright © 2023 Josephine Palermo

ISBN

Paperback: 978-1-922982-10-0
Ebook: 978-1-922982-11-7

Josephine Palermo has asserted her rights under the Copyright, Designs and Patents Act 1988 to be identified as the author of this work. The information in this book is based on the author's experiences and opinions. The publisher specifically disclaims responsibility for any adverse consequences which may result from use of the information contained herein. Permission to use information has been sought by the author. Any breaches will be rectified in further editions of the book.

All rights reserved. No part of this publication may be reproduced, stored in or introduced into a retrieval system, or transmitted in any form, or by any means (electronic, mechanical, photocopying, recording or otherwise) without the prior written permission of the author. Any person who does any unauthorised act in relation to this publication may be liable to criminal prosecution and civil claims for damages. Enquiries should be made through the publisher.

Cover design: Ultimate World Publishing
Image ©Copyright Melissa La Bozzetta 2019 - All rights reserved
Layout and typesetting: Ultimate World Publishing
Editor: Carmela Julian Valencia

Ultimate World Publishing
Diamond Creek,
Victoria Australia 3089
www.writeabook.com.au

Testimonial
☆ ☆ ☆ ☆ ☆

I would like to thank you for the opportunity to articulate my story honestly and safely. This journey of true feminine power is important. Thank you for writing this book.

With love and gratitude

Elissa

Contents

☆ ☆ ☆ ☆ ☆

Testimonial	iii
Preface	1
Introduction	3
Chapter 1: Where Did We Learn About Power	11
Chapter 2: Where Do All the Powerful Women Go?	27
Chapter 3: New Philosophy of Positive Femininity	43
Chapter 4: Playing to Your Unique Feminine Strengths	51
Chapter 5: Letting Go of Old 'Power' Beliefs	63
Chapter 6: All Girls Become Mothers, Don't They?	83
Chapter 7: Get Your Boss Pants On; We Need You	95
Chapter 8: Unleashing Your Power	103
Chapter 9: Growing Your Power	115
Chapter 10: Keep Your Power	119
Chapter 11: Let's Fix Gender Equality for Good	129
End Remarks	143
Acknowledgements	145
About The Author	149

Preface

☆ ☆ ☆ ☆ ☆

You've probably picked this book because you're curious about power. You may be curious about your power or the power someone else currently has over you. Or you may want some inspiration for growing your power and keeping it once you have it. All these things, women think about very often. We go from feeling disempowered to feeling incredibly powerful and then back again. It's like being on a power see-saw.

By the end of this book, I want you to better understand your power base and the world around you. I want you to understand the barriers that can be overcome for women around seizing power, the power you deserve, and the power that is every woman's right. The world needs more women in leadership positions and positions of power so that we can solve some of the most complex problems the planet is facing. The world needs you to step up – for your family, your children, your future self – and be the person you know you can be.

I interviewed almost 30 women while writing this book. I hope that you find as much inspiration in their stories as I did. Their stories are about how they experience power – and disempowerment – through their personal and work life and through their lives as mothers, wives, divorcees, grandmothers and all those other roles women play as leaders in their communities and at work. I have deliberately told these stories in their beautiful voices because we need to continue to hear the varied and diverse voices of women. We need to learn from each other and to keep telling each other stories about our experiences because our experiences do matter. Stories do have an impact on others, even in a small way. So, I send you this with love and a call to action. My hope and wish for you is that you are inspired to make that smallest next step into your own power.

In writing this book, my inspiration was DC Comics superhero Wonder Woman, Princess Diana of Themyscira, and her Lasso of Truth.[1] The lasso was forged by Hephaestus, the god of metalworking, therefore making it indestructible. It forces those entrapped by their own falsehoods to reveal the truth and restores lost memories. It can dispel illusions, so we see the environment for what it is and can wield our power accordingly.

So, I invite you to take a stance, put your fists on your hips, and let's channel Wonder Woman as we deconstruct what we know about power with the Lasso of Truth, and use it to understand and unveil all those things that have been hidden from us.

---

[1] American psychologist William Moulton Marston and his wife, Elizabeth Holloway, invented the early prototype of the lasso and the comic character Wonder Woman. https://en.wikipedia.org/wiki/William_Moulton_Marston.

Introduction

☆ ☆ ☆ ☆ ☆

This book is about the journey women go through to achieve true feminine power. Through stories told by women themselves, we explore how we gain power, how we lose it, how we unleash it, how we keep it and how we create magic with it. The stories told in this book are lessons learned, and some learned repeatedly. They are interspersed with some of my academic research and reading on women and power, which contextualises these lessons in knowledge from social science about how and why women use and struggle with power.

Early effects of socialisation in environments – constructed in favour of men and masculine forms of power – profoundly shape our relationship with power. The natural confidence we start with as little girls can be diluted and even lost by the time we enter puberty. A survey by the authors of The Confidence Code for Girls asked girls aged 8 to 14 to rate their confidence on a scale of 1 to 10. The average drop in perceived confidence was 30% for girls, and 'by the age of 14 the average girl was far less confident than the average boy.'[2] There are many reasons this happens. One of them is that many girls have become aware that the world still treats boys and men with privilege. I also see a drop in confidence in many young women I mentor when they suddenly hit career barriers when starting a family after a meteoric rise in career opportunities in their early years. Many of the stories told by women in this book begin with how they first became aware

---

[2] C Shipman, K Kay & J Riley, 'How Puberty Kills Girls' Confidence', The Atlantic, 2018, https://www.theatlantic.com/family/archive/2018/09/puberty-girls-confidence/563804/.

of power and how that influenced their ongoing relationship with it throughout their lives.

Before we begin to explore women's stories about their journey to true feminine power, let me define what I mean by 'power'. The challenge is that it can be defined in several ways. You can define power as an individual attribute. In other words, it's something within the person or a motivational driver. Authors like Jeffrey Pfeffer and David McClelland have defined power as an internal trait or motivational driver of our behaviour.

Others have defined power as something that is attributable to the structures in organisations and society. For example, you can have power just by the role that you currently fulfil in an organisation regardless of your internal motivation. That's positional power. We can also define power in a relational way, where power is a function of the relationships between people and these structural or organisational elements. For example, if you work in an organisation and lots of people rely on you, then you have more power than someone who isn't central to the workflow in that way. That's influential power.

I prefer to define power in a relational way. This means that power is the way we relate in our environments. It's a process, not an attribute. Power isn't a separate trait within the individual or a structure, but a relational outcome of people, groups and structures. And oftentimes, those structures are designed in a way that advantages and disadvantages certain groups of people in society. Jean Baker Miller, who wrote Toward a New Psychology of Women in 1976, defined power in this way, as the capacity to make full human development possible. Because power is relational, it is also constantly changing, being defined and redefined, depending on where your capacity resides in that society at a given moment, and what role you fulfil in relation to others. This is why we can feel and wield power very differently in an environment that's affirming and empowering for women as opposed to an environment that is not supportive. This final definition of power, to me, is the most adaptive, and responsive to change.

INTRODUCTION

Losing my sealskin

I've made it my life's work to understand, inspire and advocate for women. The reason why I've done this is that from early childhood to mid-adulthood I didn't have that inspiration myself. And so, I've always been passionate about helping women unleash their power, keep their power and focus on their unique strengths.

As a child, I had zero role models. There were no powerful women around me, in the sense that I understand power today. The women in my migrant Italian extended family used indirect power through manipulation because the men in their lives dominated them. They were passive and domesticated. Their husbands, fathers and brothers commandeered their destinies.

I saw my mother, Lina, struggle with this. If I had met my mother as a child, she would have been one of those girls that shone brightly – and she still does shine brightly, I must admit. But, I think, as a child, she would have been one of those children that stands out, with a cheeky grin, mischievous eyes and a huge curiosity and intelligence.

Yet, she was unable to fulfil that potential because of the lack of opportunity around her. My mother grew up in a village on the slopes of Mount Etna in Sicily. There was much poverty. She was a post-World War II baby – a child of a traumatised generation. Her mother never showed her any affection. Making up for that deficiency, my mother was the apple of her father's eye. They were very close. He brandished all his affection and love on her.

But then, my mother's father died when she was nine. She often retells the story of walking into her father's bedroom, where he lay on the bed, dead. It was customary in those days to keep the body in the home for days after the death of a loved one.

It was then that my mother's life changed. She had loved school but was forced to leave to help her mother look after her five brothers. Although her brothers were older, it was her obligation as the only daughter to sacrifice her needs for their needs and wants.

I think this was partly the reason she came to Australia as an 18-year-old. She took a voyage for two and a half months on a boat with her cousins and left her brothers back in Europe to find herself a better life in Australia. However, for women of her generation, part of that involved getting married and being a mother. She met my father and was married within six months.

I can imagine the struggles in their early married life. But they didn't excuse my father's behaviour. He wielded his misogynist position of power in the home from the beginning and ensured that my mother understood that she was subjugated to him. He was often violent towards her and wanted to keep her in her place.

I am sure the bright light of her childhood slowly diminished with each disappointment – the disappointment of marriage to a husband who was an alcoholic and abusive and the disappointment of the lack of support around her. She did report the domestic violence to her cousins and aunt, but they told her it was her burden to bear alone. That was the attitude of that generation and the larger Australian society at the time – they tolerated domestic violence and did not intervene. Whilst there is more awareness and proactivity today, we still see too many families continuing to experience intimate partner violence.

I was born into that family as a second child, 14 months after my sister. I kept looking at the women around me and comparing them to the men. It did not sit with me – this idea that men had control over women and that women were submissive to men. However, what I couldn't comprehend at the time were the unconscious lessons I was learning about power and women in that situation: Power is wielded indirectly. Otherwise, you get in trouble, and you get hurt. In the face of someone expressing direct power, I need to cower and be submissive. I hadn't realised it, but these are the things that I was learning about power in those early critical years.

As a young girl, one of the things that saved me was education. I always enjoyed learning and was thrilled to be at school, mainly because it gave me a reprieve from home. I loved my teachers. They were living a different life from the women in my family. I embraced school, and I was good at it. I was creative and intellectual. I studied science and arts. I did well and was able to go to university.

INTRODUCTION

I always knew I wanted to go to university, even though very few of the women and men in my family, including my extended family, had those aspirations. Many of my family members were running businesses, so there was a value placed on entrepreneurship, but no one valued education.

I curated my own educational experiences. At home, I was the person who had to translate English for my parents, so I couldn't rely on them to help me navigate my education or advise me about choosing subjects or educational pathways. Regardless, I achieved. Although my mother was very proud of my achievements, my academic achievements were made in somewhat silence because my family didn't grasp their extent.

Education was my ticket out, to a different life, so I didn't stop until I received the highest qualification: my PhD. I'm very proud of that.

On the other hand, my family couldn't understand why, at 35, I was childfree and still studying. They would say, 'You're just studying for years and years and years. What are you doing?' The fact that I was in my mid-30s and had no children was juxtaposed against this PhD I had achieved. For them, success was achieving the former, not the latter.

One of the other defining moments in my life was when, at 16, I started a relationship with someone I met in secondary school. He was my first love. I had found someone with whom I could connect with and relate to. I thought my life would be different from my parents'. What I didn't realise at the time was that what I had learned about power was now impacting the decisions I was making within my budding experience of a deep, romantic relationship. Therefore, this relationship wasn't supportive of my unique strengths.

We were both young, and I don't blame him, but I allowed myself to be subjugated, to play a less powerful role in the relationship even when I could lead rather than follow. Bit by bit – like my mother had done – my light, my cheeky smile and the twinkle in my eye were diminished with each disappointment.

When we finally broke up four and a half years later, I realised I was broken. I was no longer the confident teenager I had been when I started the relationship.

Instead, my self-esteem was damaged, as was my confidence. I felt like I had missed something in my late teen years. I had missed the opportunity to explore myself more and stayed in a relationship that required paying attention to him. What I should have known, and what I now know, is that attention flows with power. Attention will always be on the more powerful person in the relationship.

I knew I was broken. Yet, instead of working on strategies to build that power base for myself, I shut myself off from emotional connections to others to ensure that would never happen again. This had a huge impact on my life – on my two marriages and two divorces. I couldn't fully give myself to those relationships, so the result was inevitable.

During this time, I read a story that helped me find an important breakthrough. The book was Women Who Run with the Wolves by Clarissa Pinkola Estes, PhD. Dr Estes unfolds myths, fairytales, parables and her own stories that help women reconnect with their instinctual *wild woman* – the powerful force that is an ageless knowing within all women. It's beautifully written and has literally changed my life. I was given this book by a woman who owned a house overlooking a wild ocean in New Zealand. I was staying there for the weekend after my relationship breakup. After listening to me for a while, she got up, went to her bookshelf, and said, 'You need to read this.'

The story that particularly resonated with me is called 'Sealskin, Soulskin'. The story tells of a lonely hunter who wishes for a female companion to bring him happiness. One day while hunting, he spotted a small group of naked women on a rock by the sea. He inched closer and noticed sealskins on the rock nearby, so he took one.

Startled, the women who were actually seal women, grabbed the remaining sealskins and dove into the sea. All except one. She could not return to her seal form without her sealskin.

Captivated by her beauty, the man said, 'Be my wife, as I am a lonely man. I promise to return your sealskin in seven summers.' The woman reluctantly agreed, lived with the man as his wife and conceived a son. As the seventh summer neared, the

INTRODUCTION

woman began to tire, her flesh began to dry out, and her once luscious hair began to fall to the floor. She begged for her sealskin back, but the man became enraged and hid it. After witnessing his mother's continued suffering, her little boy found the sealskin and returned it to his mother. While, of course, sad to leave the man and her son, the woman realised that she must go back to the sea. Immediately as the cold water surrounded her, she found her beauty and vitality return.

This story resonated with me at the time because my own sealskin was gone. Like the woman in the story, my health was deteriorating. I had a damaging immune response to all sorts of allergens, which rendered me extremely ill for over a year. I was allergic to foods, pollen, dust and many other environmental factors. My symptoms were chronic hay fever, asthma and eczema that would plague me from head to toe. When I had a bad episode, my eczema would come up like hives and then dry out, and my skin would peel right off. When I heard the story of the sealskin woman, I knew it was me. My sealskin had been stolen. My essence, the things that make me uniquely me, was gone. And so, from there I took a road to self-discovery and healing. I made lots of mistakes along the way and moved forward into a more authentic life, step by step.

This book is my gift to you. It's my gift to women impacted by the imbalance in power due to their gender, race and abilities. It is my gift to you if you envisage a world where we value a different type of femininity: A positive femininity that is powerful rather than passive, where masculinity and femininity are in balance, and one is not subjugated by the other.

Chapter 1

Where Did We Learn About Power

☆ ☆ ☆ ☆ ☆

As women living and acting in the world, we are all confronted by the social systems that either constrain us or help us flourish. There are barriers we face from people who want to or do have power over us, people we have power over and people we share power with. Along the way, we may gain and lose power, or struggle to maintain and keep it.

Power is relational. It's an attribute of our relationship with other people, and it shifts and changes according to the status of our relationships and the conditions in our environments.

What I learned about power in my younger years did not set me up well to navigate the world. I had to overcome parts of my story to do that successfully (which I'll share more of throughout this book).

In writing this book, I was interested in how other women have learned about power as they journey through their lives. The different beliefs about power and why some women differ in their beliefs struck me. The stories in this chapter explore when women discovered their power base and the forces at play that created different beliefs.

Nicole: Exploring my progress in power – it's complicated

Nicole has many interesting stories to tell, collected from an enthralling life. She is a film producer and director who, after spending more than a decade in the Kimberley with the indigenous people of that land, produced an award-winning feature-length documentary called Putuparri and the Rainmakers. This and other accomplishments have culminated in a successful career in the arts that spans decades. Yet, Nicole is ambivalent about her own power.

> *There are days you get up and feel really powerful. Other days I might be doing something simple that I know I can do, and I fall apart. I don't think it's something you can just tell yourself and believe. You could say, 'I'm powerful. I'm a powerful woman.' But I think we are a mess of contradictions.*
>
> *I'm a woman of colour. I'm Chinese. Now I'm examining and exploring myself as a woman of colour, and I'm cognisant that you're a white woman questioning me as a coloured woman.*
>
> *I'm exploring my progression in the power structures and hierarchies within my own culture. For me, it's very complicated. Sometimes I feel very powerful, and I don't give a shit. I will think I can do what I want to do. And then, a lot of times, I feel totally insignificant, and my self-esteem is zero; negative. And I can't do anything; I'm frozen. It depends on so many outside influences, internal influences and how I look or don't look at that time. Yeah, it's complicated.*

Women have been socialised into the belief that power is not naturally theirs to hold. This is often in response to forms of power that come from a masculine or agentic (individualist) view of self that they reject or see as more an attribute of men rather than women.

Through early childhood experiences, women learn that certain psychological attributes are associated with being male and others with being female. In fact, this is a construction or a shared belief our societal system then reinforces and maintains.

Beulah meets Buffy the Vampire Slayer

I met Beulah many years ago, when she and her soon-to-be husband were performing world music in a band called Jadidah. Beulah has a beautiful voice and her daughter has followed in her parents' creative footsteps. Now in her 40s, Beulah is a Senior Manager in an employee psychological assistance practice after having completed a PhD in Psychology. Many years before all that, Beulah was raised in a patriarchal Sri Lankan Indian family. Losing both her parents at a very early age forced her to make some life-changing decisions.

In Sri Lankan Indian culture, the males are the ones who are the cherished, valued members of the family, and the women are the servants. Essentially, you do things to help the men feel better about themselves.

Yes, you give up things for the men.

Women create power by seeming powerless, when in fact they are the hidden matriarchs of the family who do have decision-making powers. For most women in my family, that sense of powerlessness just crushed them.

It became an environment where people scrambled for power and held it over other people, without necessarily being conscious of it all the time. It was not uncommon for the sons and fathers to take advantage of that dynamic to get what they wanted when they wanted things.

As a young child in Singapore, where I grew up, I had no power. I think children don't tend to have any power. The adults are the ones with power in that relationship. But another layer on top of that was the unhealthiness going on around me: I was powerless in a horrible situation, which got worse after both my parents died, and there was no exit. So, I learned how to become invisible and hide and be the person who made the peace with everybody.

I was that person who smoothed things over and made things easier for everybody. Because I wasn't really respected or acknowledged as a person of value, I learned to hide in the shadows. And that created a lot of problems down the track for me, in some ways.

As a teenager, of course, you do push and pull a lot more. And there was some of that happening. It got to the stage where I had to make the decision to leave Singapore and start off on my own without my extended family. That was probably the first step for me to come into my own power, by removing myself at that age, argue and fight for the chance to extract myself from that situation and start anew.

My first memory of power – and this is funny – was when I started watching Buffy the Vampire Slayer, which is a TV series that aired from 1997 to 2003. Buffy is this tiny blonde girl who beats the crap out of bad vampires. When I saw that, I was a bit gobsmacked that a woman could be that strong. I'm still a fan of Buffy. That was really one of the first times I thought maybe I could actually beat the crap out of stuff I've experienced.

Seeing a female character be that way opened my eyes. I had no clue that I had power at all. I struggled so much with my internal self-talk because I was not there yet, but that did start raising the veil from my eyes – maybe life could be different as a woman, in work and my personal life.

Rachel and the frowny-faced nun

Rachel is a mother of three children, entrepreneur, life coach, author, facilitator and speaker who is passionate about inspiring people, especially children and the adults who surround them, to reach their full potential in life. Rachel has worked extensively in education, delivering professional learning and coaching related to life skills and parent engagement. She has also recently published her book to support parents as they guide and support their children's learning journey.

Rachel describes herself as a one-time introvert who, over the years, has developed a more extroverted leadership style. Her early experiences of powerlessness may have planted the seed that led to a successful career helping parents better connect with their children's learning journey.

In primary school, I was taught by nuns, and some of them were lovely. In contrast, some were harsh and really nasty to kids.

This particular nun always had a frown on her face. I was always terrified of her. Being quite timid and shy, I was going through some tough times at home because my parents had separated; none of the teachers knew. In addition, I had lost my best friend because she moved away. No one really told kids anything back then, so I didn't even know where she had moved to. As a kid, I just thought she's gone, she's just gone. So, my young brain was thinking, 'Oh, everyone just leaves.'

One particular incident at school got me into terrible trouble with the nun. I had lost a library book and was trying to explain to her that I had looked everywhere for it and couldn't find it. That wasn't good enough for the frowny-faced nun. She put me at the front of the class and rapped my knuckles with a ruler. The tears streamed down my face. It wasn't that it hurt. It was my pride. Because it was humiliating. Absolutely humiliating. I've always remembered that. It was probably one of the first times I wasn't listened to, and so I retreated into my shell for several years.

Melanie gives away her power

Melanie has achieved a successful career as a Senior Project Manager in IT. She is articulate, bright and lights up a room when she enters it. She has two young children and a loving husband. But before all that, she was navigating power in a very abusive relationship.

I was with my ex-partner for 10 years, and it was an abusive relationship. It started quite simply – just little comments to put you down, make you feel bad. Then, it escalated over the years to emotional and physical abuse. By the end of that relationship, I knew I had no power. In fact, I tried to take my power back – and it's embarrassing to say this – by asking him to marry me. It was normal for me. When I was in that relationship, normal was him having me in a headlock against a wall. So, if he wasn't doing that one day, we were good. That's why I felt it was okay to ask him to marry me. I asked him to marry me, and he said no.

At the time, I remember driving around, then sitting in the car park until about three or four in the morning, bawling my eyes out because I had the realisation that my life was a complete mess. I had just asked this man to marry me because I wanted to take some power back, and that had backfired. I didn't know what to do. I was too afraid to move on. But he did do me a favour because that just reset me. Even though I still didn't have the power or the strength to leave at that point, I was able to distance myself. That gave me perspective, which then allowed me to return to my family.

I didn't feel strong enough to stand up then, but I was able to leave, which was a big step for me. It took time, but looking back on that whole part of my life, one of the hardest things I've ever done was leave that relationship. It was easier to stay. That sounds horrible, but when you're in there, the fear and the different emotions you feel when you leave are overwhelming – it's just horrible.

Looking back, that experience gave me stronger values and resilience. And it's given me perspective. I don't think I would be the person I am today without going through that. I don't mean this in a bad way, but I was arrogant and a little bit spoiled. I brought a lot of attention to myself being petite and blonde, and I had not experienced being alone. Going through that experience taught me lessons about who I am as a person, what I want from my life, and what I will tolerate and what I will not. Having said that, I'm glad I got out, and I'm glad no children were involved. It was a real turning point in my life.

Gwen: I peaked when I was four!

Gwen, in her late 30s, has a spark in her eye and exuberance that fills a room. She loves her close-knit group of friends and is global in her outlook. Gwen is passionate about women's empowerment and believes everyone has the right to shine in their own way. She diligently worked her way up the hierarchy in her consulting firm, eventually making partner, only to discover some hard truths about her colleagues and the organisation she worked in once she joined their leadership ranks.

I peaked when I was four! I can remember that was the time when I felt I fit in the world. I had anything I wanted. I had amazing dresses; I had amazing shoes. Everybody loved me. It was a fantastic life! Every 4-year-old, probably within reason, has that sort of feeling of confidence. But then, what happens after that?

There were some surprising realisations when I was going through the partnership process, as the process presents a lot of challenging questions, such as 'What sets you apart?' and 'What do you want to be known for?'

I had a lot of self-doubt, lacking confidence in whether I even had what it takes to be successful. It dawned on me that I used to be so self-assured, so confident, and knew how to take on the world … when I was 4 years old.

If I think about my education and upbringing, subtly I was taught to 'fit in', to 'be like everyone'. For a child who has always been different – I have mixed heritage, and so I didn't really fit in most places – it has dominated my life for as long as I can remember. Even working in a bank at the beginning of my career, I remember being told that I was 'too bubbly' or that I 'lacked gravitas'. I had to look up what gravitas meant at that point! Despite that, I was a good student and I took my development seriously. I put my head down and worked hard. I trained away the things that made me different, so I could succeed. And I internalised that journey.

What has always been interesting to me is that as we become leaders, we have to embrace what sets us apart. The way I managed to empower myself was to remember what it felt like when I was 4 years old. I shone like a star, so I told myself, 'You've got it in you. You've felt like that before, and you can shine again.'

Angelique decides to live by her own rules

Angelique is a successful HR Director with a long career in manufacturing organisations and other male-dominated industries. She is passionate and outspoken, advocating for the people in her organisation with confidence and strength whilst, at the same time, being comfortable with being vulnerable. Through her career and life journey, she realised that the power structures she had been raised in no longer served her.

Growing up in Malta, in a traditional patriarchal family, my father never missed an opportunity to tell me that he was the man of the house and that 'you live by my rules'.

I could understand it was power, but I knew it was bigger than me. At the same time, it never sat right with me. I wasn't one of those traditional submissive females. I always questioned it. Why does it have to be like this? Why is it always his way or the highway?

I always wanted to leave Malta. But there was never the right time. My mother passed away at the age of 48. She was so very young. I had to step up – to be my dad's 'wife', my brother's 'mum' and all that jazz. I was only in my late teens at the time, and I was putting my dreams on hold, and that still wasn't making my dad happy. So, I decided it was time to take the reins and do what I wanted. I told my dad I was going away for five years initially. With my husband at the time, we decided to come to Australia. That's when my dad learned that I wasn't ever going back home.

Cindy: Deep-seated unworthiness

Cindy is a beautiful and wise woman. As a successful Entrepreneur and Business Consultant for many years, she stepped into her power after being diagnosed with breast cancer for the second time.

I feel like I've been someone my whole life whom, on the exterior, everyone would say, 'Oh, you seem so confident; you're a great speaker.'

But on the inside, it was a very different story.

For my whole adult life, I've had opportunities to speak up. Speaking is a way to demonstrate your power in alignment with who you are and what you have to say in the world. But at the same time, I've always had huge resistance to thinking of myself as powerful. It wasn't until I had breast cancer the second time that I felt something clicked. I can now speak with confidence, volition and alignment that I have something worthwhile to say.

The first time I went through breast cancer, I was in complete denial. It was so much easier to focus on work, my son, my responsibilities. I didn't share my diagnosis or struggles with many people. I hid myself away. I thought I needed to do it on my own. My work colleagues didn't even know what I was going through.

I refused most of the treatment the doctors recommended. In many ways I was thinking, I'm so important. My business needed me. My clients needed me. And so, there was a bit of martyrdom.

But looking back now, it was crazy to think that I couldn't stop, that I needed to keep going and that everybody else's needs were more important than my own. I didn't have time to put myself and my needs first – or so I thought. I didn't even want to take time out for treatment. I placed more value on keeping busy and didn't allow time for my health. At the core of it, I didn't want to disappoint others.

Even in the midst of my own mess, I felt a sense of obligation to others rather than my own needs. I would never recommend this approach to others, but that is what I prioritised for myself. I was very much in my ego, desperately clutching on to my business persona and others' perception of me. It didn't come from a place of love, I can assure you, it was bullshit. At the very core, I've got some deep-seated unworthiness issues. I grew up in a family where I was the eldest of four girls. There was pressure on me to be a good girl, to do well at school, to be a great role model, and to be a good citizen.

My mother, in particular, was very critical. Even though I was a straight-A student, played on the sports teams, never touched drugs, didn't party or drink excessively, I was criticised no matter what. So, I felt like I could never do anything right.

I once got a Good Citizenship award, which was a huge honour at school. I thought, 'Wow, I must be a good person.' But at the same time, I also questioned that.

Getting cancer for the second time was a big part of stripping back those layers of BS I've been wearing for so long, trying to be something I wasn't. I guess that's the consolation, isn't it? Cancer strips you bare, and you think, 'Fuck it! Life's too short. I haven't got time to try being anything or anyone but me.'

Harb and the funeral pyre

Harb achieved the coveted Arts Editor job at a major Australian newspaper after working as a journalist in Malaysia and then Melbourne. After she had been living in Australia for several years, she returned to Malaysia to attend her father's funeral.

We placed my father's body on a stack of wood at the funeral site. When you set fire to a body, sometimes the spine can shrink and the body can sit up. So, you must place wood on top of it to avoid that.

My brother went to my father, took his hand, took the watch my father had given him, and put it on his own wrist. And then he lit the funeral pyre.

Women traditionally didn't go to these rituals, but I wanted to be there. I was standing quite close to the funeral pyre. It hit me at that moment that the body was just the body, that he was no longer there.

One of my uncles tried to shield my face from this and grabbed my arm. I told him to let go. I wanted to be there in my full presence. Life and death hit me at that moment, and I realised there was no time to waste.

When I came back to Australia, I left my marriage. I realised just how much I had compromised myself. Although I was dynamic, bright, positive, driven and doing well in the journalistic arena, I felt I had given away something of myself. I had given away my power. My father's death shifted that for me. It was almost like a gift he gave me.

I began years of therapy and looked at the kind of dysfunctions in the family and how I had stepped up to play particular roles – I was the family cheerleader because my mother was depressed. As a child, the dynamic operating was that if I were available to cheer my mother up, she would take care of me.

Then, there was my father, a traditional Indian man who was quite emotionally distant. Not that he wasn't loving, but it was an undemonstrative kind of love. So, I ended up being attracted to men whom I had to fix or who were distant, neither of which I was in my power with.

I spent years grieving, letting go, coming into my power and understanding myself better. My full name Harbant means 'disciple of the truth'. I don't know if that's where it comes from, but I've always been curious. I used to read seven books a week when I was a kid. I've always been interested in other people's lives, which is what led me to journalism, I think.

How we see power can affect the way we move towards it or avoid it. Women sometimes shy away from hierarchical forms of power because, stereotypically, that's not aligned with doing good for others: their families, their community, their workplace and their colleagues.

Women's sense of connection or communion may act against their desire for power over others. But, this doesn't mean that women do not desire power to make an impact on others. This is power **with** rather than power **over** others. The problem is that this form of power isn't aligned with what is valued most in the familial, social and cultural systems we grew up in, at home and work, and is therefore denigrated to a weaker, less attractive form of power.

In our early years, we miss the opportunity to see the value that communal power creates because attention flows upwards. We learn to give our attention to those more powerful. In doing so, we attribute men with masculinity and power.[3] We value the form of power that men demonstrate, which this is often power over others. This is best illustrated with the story of the Elephant and the Mouse.

---

[3] E Stamkou, G van Kleef, A Fischer, & M Kret, 'Are the Powerful Really Blind to the Feelings of Others? How Hierarchical Concerns Shape Attention to Emotions', Personality & social psychology bulletin, vol 42(6), 2016, pp 755–768, https://pubmed.ncbi.nlm.nih.gov/27036499/.

In an old African fable[4], the mouse builds her nest on the ground, only to have the large elephant crush it every night under its foot without even noticing. So, the mouse builds another nest the next day, only to have the same thing happen. The mouse decides that to survive in this environment with the elephant, she will need to learn everything about the other. She will need to be aware of his likes, dislikes, moods and behaviours to keep out of the elephant's way and avoid getting crushed by a wayward step.

In this fable, the elephant is a metaphor for the most dominant group in any system or environment, such as family structures and workplaces, biased towards masculinity. Because of their sheer size and force, they can go through life without a second thought to the much smaller and weaker mouse. The elephant doesn't need to understand the mouse or adapt his behaviour to her needs and desires. On the other hand, the mouse is acutely aware of the elephant's presence and needs to know everything about it to survive.

We often see highly competent women feeling like they must be twice as good as the men around them to be noticed for promotion. They need to know how to adapt to the climate and circumstances in male-dominated roles and highly masculine workplace cultures. And because the system that both men and women work in is biased towards masculinity, it favours a workforce that work full-time and don't have caring responsibilities.

The global COVID-19 pandemic accelerated trends in flexibility. It showed on a global scale that we can have flexible working arrangements and give more autonomy to workers about when and where work is performed without any loss of productivity. Yet, even after all that, as soon as public health restrictions were lifted, most employers and leaders resolved to bring everyone back to the office, whilst most workers did not want to return to those norms of the past (that favour traditional masculine stereotypes).

We must rethink the masculine version of power and embrace a more connected version. Power is not a dirty word. Like money, it is not inherently evil. What

---

[4] The Mouse and the Elephant – An African Fable, Indigo Sea Press Blog, 2014, https://secondwindpub.wordpress.com/2014/04/24/the-mouse-and-the-elephant-an-african-fable/.

if we defined power with positive femininity? What would that look like in our work and life?

In our reconceptualisation of power, we need a way that goes beyond rejecting traditional forms of power. Instead, we need to think about the driver for our human evolution as one that leads to balance between masculine and feminine forms of power.

From a very early age, as early as infancy, boys are socialised into independence and individualism. They see themselves as separate from their environment and are encouraged to stand out, be competitive, speak up and be assertive, finding reward in being independent from their environment rather than connected to it. You can think of this as 'agency'.

Girls, on the other hand, are socialised into being connected with their environment. That communal orientation makes them more aware of others around them, empathic to others' feelings and gives them a sense of themselves as part of an ecosystem. So, they're encouraged to nurture, be considerate of others, be helpful and agreeable and have empathy. You can think of this as 'communion'.

For women, this sense of being connected while being a strength may impair their ability to be independent. For men, this sense of being independent while also a strength may impair their ability to be connected. Therefore, men's evolutionary driver is to connect to communion and femininity. Equally, for women, it is to connect to agency and masculinity. The developmental arcs that men and women must journey are integral to providing a world of balance where all human beings express both masculinity and femininity in environments that enable both to flourish.[5]

Gwen rejects masculine forms of power

I joined the Mentoring Program conducted by the Women's Foundation in Hong Kong in 2016. It was a life-changing program for me. As part of that program,

---

[5] These concepts are expanded on in David Bakan's The Duality of Human Existence: Isolation and Communion in Western Man, Beacon Press, 1966.

we had lots of workshops and lectures and sessions in addition to the one-to-one mentoring relationship, which is a much-valued relationship in my life so many years later.

One of the sessions I remember clearly was on power. I attended with my mentor who thought it was a brilliant breakdown of power. The speaker's key idea was that because power is like a web, you need to understand where these webs are so that you stand in the right place.

While my mentor really loved the lecture, I didn't relate to it at all. It was almost like words were just flying by me.

As I read and understand more about power, I realise that it's not something I can relate to. In my mind, I like to build community. I love my team. How we work and play together is important in terms of morale and energy. I care deeply about the people I work with, and I want to make sure we are all happy to be where we are. Ideas such as having power over other people or basing influence on hierarchy are not as relatable to me. But it wasn't foreign to the leaders around me. During the partner process, my mentors were telling me that I need to learn how to play the game.

I've always had an interest in people. One of my favourite books on this topic is Cassandra Speaks: When Women Are the Storytellers, the Human Story Changes by Elizabeth Lesser. She says that the way we think about power is so masculine. That's why, as women, it's hard to relate to power in that way. We need to start rephrasing power and the way we understand it.

This book moved me to tears, as it encapsulates how I think about power so well. These concepts opened a whole new world to me. In fact, the chapter that made me cry was about speaking up and finding your voice. Women are told that they speak too much. It reminded me that, as a child, I'd always been told that. Yet, research has shown that men speak much more than women, especially in public spaces. The book explained that women talking to each other is how we influence the world around us, how women get things done. I will be forever grateful to Elizabeth Lesser for articulating what power means for me.

Aung San Suu Kyi famously said, 'It is not power that corrupts but fear. Fear of losing power corrupts those who wield it. Fear of the scourge of power corrupts those who are subject to it.'[6]

Balancing power requires those who wield power to let go of it and those who are subject to power to embrace it. There are genuine barriers to women achieving power, which go beyond their beliefs about power. In the next chapter, we explore some of these barriers.

---

[6] Aung San Suu Kyi's written speech for the Sakharov Prize for Freedom of Thought in 1990, Germany, https://speakola.com/political/aung-san-suu-kyi-freedom-from-fear-1990.

Chapter 2

Where Do All the Powerful Women Go?

☆ ☆ ☆ ☆ ☆

Aren't you sick of all the Johns and Daves in leadership positions? CEOs named John or Dave outnumber women in leadership positions across the C-Suite in the USA.[7] At the same time, current role models for young, ambitious women are, in the main, Instagram celebrities.

Whilst they are getting somewhat closer to what positive femininity could be, their avatars send mixed messages about beauty and power, which leaves us, ordinary women, feeling like power is beyond us (unless we have the necessary surgical enhancements or starve ourselves to achieve an unachievable beauty norm). In real life, there's a dearth of strong female role models in positions of power and leadership that portray true feminine power.

---

[7] M Liddy & C Hanrahan, 'Fewer women run top Australian companies than men named John. Or Peter. Or David', ABC News, 2017, https://www.abc.net.au/news/2017-03-08/fewer-women-ceos-than-men-named-john/8327938.

The lack of role models bothered me for many years in my early career. I hadn't met anyone in leadership who resembled me. It was only when I was in my late twenties that I met the first Italian woman who held a leadership position. She was a Director in a federal government department. I was awestruck because I had never seen anyone like me in leadership. When we never see our likeness in the leaders around us, we're never given a chance to imagine ourselves in that role, whereas men, especially white men, see that all the time.

I was stunned to meet this stylishly dressed woman with her Italian accent. She had a slight frame, like all the Italian women I know in my extended family, but the difference was that she was in a leadership position and was doing it with great command and grace. She used direct language in the way she led – she commandeered the room. I just loved being around her. But, in some ways, it was jarring because I hadn't realised what I was missing until I saw her.

In my career as a senior leader, it took me a long time to discover how to be authentic and which battles were worth fighting for and which weren't. I often felt like a square peg being shoved into a round hole. I didn't realise that the shape of the hole was wrong. In my uniqueness, I was perfectly fit for leadership. Yet, the leadership stereotypes didn't fit the positive feminine qualities I wanted to express.

Femininity, as defined in psychology, is a gender identity, or internalised cognitive schema, that comprises negative and positive traits. Gender is formed in an iterative process with society, where individuals understand themselves and their relationships with others and society along a continuum of femininity and masculinity. Negative feminine traits include submissiveness and passivity, whereas positive feminine traits include empathy, nurturance and collective leadership.

In studies I performed as part of my PhD, I found that whilst women could display both masculine and feminine traits in their leadership, they faced marginality and barriers to their success due to a lack of nurturance and empathy in the organisational cultures they worked within. Instead, these cultures were biased toward masculine traits, like dominance and aggressiveness, and women were not encouraged to step outside their traditional gender roles.

Women in the spotlight

Where did all the powerful women go, and why don't they put themselves out there? Did I mention earlier that attention follows power? Well, when women do step up, that attention can be used by others to the woman's detriment. As achievements of successful women are highlighted, every nuance is also noted and every mistake is amplified, more so for women leaders than men.

We have seen examples where the spotlight does not go well for women. Think back to Julia Gillard's term as Australia's first female Prime Minister. Not only was Ms Gillard a woman, but she was also unmarried and in a de facto relationship with no children – taking her outside of the more traditional stereotypical role expectations for women in society. Ms Gillard often rallied against the misogynistic views of then Federal Opposition Leader Tony Abbott. These are her words in the now-famous misogyny speech:

> *He has said, and I quote, in a discussion about women being under-represented in institutions of power in Australia, the interviewer was a man called Stavros. The Leader of the Opposition says, 'If it's true, Stavros, that men have more power generally speaking than women, is that a bad thing?'*
>
> *And then a discussion ensues, and another person says, 'I want my daughter to have as much opportunity as my son.' To which the Leader of the Opposition says 'Yeah, I completely agree, but what if men are by physiology or temperament, more adapted to exercise authority or to issue command?'*
>
> *Then ensues another discussion about women's role in modern society, and the other person participating in the discussion says, 'I think it's very hard to deny that there is an underrepresentation of women,' to which the Leader of the Opposition says, 'But now, there's an assumption that this is a bad thing.'*[8]

---

[8] J Gillard, The Misogyny Speech, speech transcript, 2012, https://www.smh.com.au/politics/federal/transcript-of-julia-gillards-speech-20121010-27c36.html; https://www.juliagillard.com.au/the-misogyny-speech/

Sue is impacted by the organisational culture

Sue is an experienced human resources consultant, having worked across various industries in her long and esteemed career. She is gentle, nurturing and caring, and has a brilliant analytical mind. In her early job experiences she was confronted with the impacts of workplace cultures that are biased towards masculinity, which ultimately led to a decision to leave organisations altogether.

My first paid job was when I was about 15 or 16 years old. I had a holiday job, cleaning shelves in a pharmacy. That's when I became aware of the boss dynamic; that I was there to serve my manager. I came across negative power more than positive power in workplaces I experienced in my early life.

At another job in the early or mid-80s, there was an incident. I was studying at university and had just lost my father to smoking. So I was outwardly anti-smoking. Yet the manager put me next to smokers. I protested to the leadership and said, 'Look, I can't work in this environment. I need to be moved away from the smokers and placed somewhere else.'

But they refused to compromise.

There was an attitude of 'We've done it this way for however many years. You can't change things.' That, to me, was a negative use of power. I took the earliest opportunity to leave that job. Luckily I came into some money from my great aunt, so I went travelling and escaped.

I suppose I've always had an attitude that if I'm not happy in one circumstance, I'll either try to solve it or move on. I have experienced negative power many times, which is probably why I'm self-employed now. I've experienced negative power in organisations – particularly, large organisations – that are significantly male-dominated, where I've experienced bullying and sexism. And it's not just the men; sometimes, women have sexist beliefs as well.

That's one of the reasons I don't like being in organisations anymore – because of that energy. It was that masculine energy that had an adverse impact on me.

I find them very draining, and I experienced burnout on a couple of occasions. Being in an organisation, to me, is negative.

We don't have enough women leaders in organisations, and the ecosystem isn't conducive to thriving. At one point, I thought it would be great to be Head of Human Resources, but when I had that role, I hated it. It nearly destroyed my marriage. I was working 60 to 80 hours a week and travelling so much. The money was nice, but the other costs were very high.

The problem is integral to the way jobs are designed. Society assumes that your value is about how hard you work and how busy you are rather than what you achieve or that you can achieve it differently.

Now I'm much stronger in saying that health is my number one priority. If I don't stay healthy, nothing else will work.

Angelique: Too aggressive, too direct

Angelique worked in traditionally male-dominated industries for many years. Like myself, she experienced her own version of being a square peg in a round hole.

It was 2010 when I started going into predominantly male industries, working in tyres. Instinctively, I committed to not showing myself as weak. I wanted a seat at the table like everyone else. I'm smart like everyone else, and I thought I will show it.

It was probably a bit too much, and I started to hear feedback that I was too aggressive or too direct. That's when I began to question myself. I started becoming a bit more introspective and reflective.

All the while, I was trying to establish myself as a leader and establish an HR function for the first time. It wasn't easy. In time, the real me started to surface, and I was demanding more of myself, saying, 'Why is it that everybody can have their say and I can't have mine?'

Establishing an HR function and dealing with soft people issues in a predominantly male environment had a double layer. If I were a female leader in supply chain or finance, I'd have a different experience yet again. Those things are more valued and aligned with the language the male executives understand, like hard numbers and facts. So, I had to sell my worth and value even before I started to speak up.

Dina: The system is biased against women

Dina is an Organisational Psychologist, Talent Strategist and Diversity & Inclusion Manager. With more than 12 years of industry experience across public, private and not-for-profit sectors, she has successfully led solutions in talent acquisition, talent development, diversity and inclusion, culture change and transformation, organisational design and capability development. She balances family life with young children and a drive to succeed in her chosen career.

In workplaces, bias shows up in those signature moments we're more likely to notice when we begin our immersion into a new culture. Dina started in a new role as Head of Diversity and Inclusion at a large corporation and immediately experienced instances of bias.

> *One instance was in the recruitment space. We were considering a person for a senior executive role who came through the whole rigmarole of the interview process. The lead hirer loved this candidate, but their psychometric profile was a red flag and a genuine concern for me on many levels. Yet, my concern got thrown out because the lead hirer wanted this person purely based on their experience and CV and because they had built rapport with the key stakeholder during the interview process.*
>
> *I've seen that situation play out so many times when it's a male candidate. But when it's a female candidate, she's immediately out of the process. It's like they'll take any excuse to eliminate a female candidate when it's a senior role, but there's more sympathy going on when it's a male.*
>
> *What I see a lot in the industries is leaders trying to meet gender equality in team structures, but that all goes out the window when changes occur for one reason or the other and the cards are then stacked against women again.*

For example, you can have a number of prominent women leave an organisation and have those roles replaced by excellent internal male candidates, which is a success story for them because they are promoted on merit. However, you're back to where you were before you started the whole drive to get more women into senior roles. It's a failure of the pipeline because we don't have the women in succession plans that can maintain the level of gender equality in those senior teams.

It's at that point that I think we've got a lot of work to do. There's a lot of opportunity for change, but I also realise it's a hard road ahead.

Harb discovers Australian Dinosaurs

Being new to the country and new in her job at the Herald Sun and later The Age newspaper, Harb described her first experience in an Australian newsroom.

It was a male-dominated newsroom. The shaming of women, the way Julia Gillard was treated, the boys' network – I thought it's just endemic to Australia.

When I was working in Malaysia, women and men were more equal. In Australia I was the only woman at the daily news conference at the Herald Sun, so it felt like a step backwards. It has progressed since then. The Age got its first woman editor recently after 160 years!

It's not that they aren't brilliant women; it's the culture. When I came to Australia and joined the newsroom, it was mainly men. It was a shock. I had the confidence young women have. I had that big vision of youth and thought I was in command, immune from those forces in the culture and my environment, even though I was a minority – a Punjabi Malaysian woman – who walked into the newsroom. At The Age, I was the only coloured person at a newspaper that is supposed to be communicating effectively to a diverse audience.

Pauline hits a glass ceiling

Pauline (not her real name) is the CEO & Managing Director of a financial services company. She is an experienced financial services leader with a demonstrated history of working in the insurance and financial advice industry. She is a charismatic leader with a deep understanding of people and culture within business. Pauline had an accelerated career from the start, finding her feet as a graduate in a competitive industry, making it all the way to National Sales Manager and then CEO. But her journey was not always smooth sailing.

> *I suppose just being a woman in this industry was a challenge. Straight away, my mentors and managers would tell me I didn't have natural leadership skills. What I did have going for me was that I could influence people. I was always the one to stand up and speak out or get something going. People started noticing me, which was great. And then, I was lucky enough to have managers who were emotionally intelligent, kind, generous and didn't have a bias against women. So, they promoted me.*

> *After a while, I came to a point where I hit that glass ceiling. At the time, I came to a juncture in my career where it was between myself and this guy who was going for a very senior position. It was a position that would have springboarded me into CEO roles within Australia or even overseas.*

> *I remember speaking to a board member about it. He said to me, 'You are a very good leader, there's no doubt about that. However, as a female, I know your priorities are going to be around wanting to start and build a family.'*

> *I didn't have children at that time. I was in my twenties, and my priorities were far from having a family and children. So, it was interesting that suddenly – after being lifted and promoted a number of times in the organisation – I got slapped down. That was my first experience of the glass ceiling.*

We know that discrimination and sexual harassment are prevalent in workplaces today. Discrimination and sexual harassment are barriers for many women – who are more likely to experience incidences along with people in other marginalised groups such as the LGBTQI+ community, people with disabilities and people in insecure work. People in marginal groups are also less likely to report discrimination and sexual harassment for fear of risking their jobs and careers.

According to Work Safe Australia, 1 in 3 people have experienced sexual harassment at work in the last five years, the majority being women.[9] It is not surprising, then, that many of the women's stories in this book also describe these experiences.

Rachel: A culture of sexual harassment

It was a horrible experience. There was an incident where a male staff member made an advancement towards a female staff member. He had attempted to do the same with me, and I saw him do it to other girls as well. Another girl and I reported him, but our opinion wasn't listened to.

At the time, we were told by the Senior Manager, 'Yes, we've heard these stories before. But he's one of our most experienced managers, so we won't take it any further.'

My early work experiences with dominant male managers almost forced me to work for myself because I didn't have many positive experiences.

Justine, on navigating poor behaviour

Justine is determined and driven. She has practised law, held multiple senior HR leadership roles, and is the author of Connect Better Faster and On the Same Page: 5 Conversations Leading for Top Team Cultures. She is the founder of a flourishing HR Executive Community and a sought-after coach.

Justine speaks frankly about being put in a difficult situation in her early career by a senior colleague. She doesn't attribute this to her gender. However, she suggests that being a woman made responding assertively especially challenging.

---

[9] Infographic on workplace sexual harassment by Safe Work Australia, https://www.safework-australia.gov.au/safety-topic/hazards/workplace-sexual-harassment.

Earlier in my career, a male senior co-worker drove me to a business meeting. It was a boozy lunch that was several hundred kilometres away from the office. During the lunch, my co-worker proceeded to get very drunk. By the end, it was clear that he couldn't drive safely. However, he insisted he was totally fine and would take me back to the office with him.

I was worried about my job security. I was still very new and trying to prove myself. I didn't feel safe getting into the car, but I also didn't feel safe to speak up. So, I decided that the best thing to do was to take the risk and get in the car with him. I respected myself less for not speaking up, and it left a bad taste in my mouth for a while.

I consider myself a particularly courageous person who doesn't back down from the hard stuff. But that day I froze. You could say it wasn't about gender. That co-worker drinking at the lunch just wanted a good time.

The challenge is that when poor behaviour happens, women react from a place where they have been socialised to smile and keep the peace. It's expected of us, or ingrained in us, in a way that is not the same for our male counterparts. Responding with true assertiveness when you're in a difficult situation can be especially challenging as a woman in a professional environment.

Pauline stands up to sexual harassment

Do you remember Pauline? She's a CEO now, driven and incredibly smart, and the most compassionate leader I know. She cares about people and has taken that into her leadership authentically throughout her career as she's progressed from Manager to executive role. When Pauline was a Sales Executive for a multinational company, she faced a situation that ran contrary to her values. She decided she needed to do something because staying silent was no longer an option.

It was the CEO. He did it very subtly. Not with me, though. He never harassed me because I was in a senior position. Instead, he preyed on the younger women in the organisation. Some of these women were in management positions as well.

One woman approached me after a Christmas party. She was in tears. Some of my peers had congregated around her, saying, 'You didn't hear what you think you heard.' They were trying to diminish it and attempting to influence her. The executives tried to cover it all up. It was disgusting!

The woman approached me and asked, 'What do I do?'

I recommended she put a complaint to HR. I said, 'I'll help you do it.'

But she wasn't willing to put in a formal complaint, so I did it on her behalf. I put it in writing with the help of a legal firm. It went to the CEO, the entire leadership team and the global head office.

At that time, I thought that was the right thing to do. I was in my power and the only female executive. I was going to do the right thing by her and all these other women. But as the issue progressed, it started unravelling.

As the finger started getting pointed at the CEO and the other executives, it all started flipping. They started saying, 'Look at what you are doing to us! You are hurting our team.' I was hit with this every day.

Consequently, I started losing my power, and the executive team appealed to me as the victims in all of this. Everything got flipped on its head, and I lost more power. It impacted me mentally and physically. That was when I decided to leave. I was unravelling myself. That scared me because I started questioning myself: Had I done the wrong thing?

So, I left and went to another company. To my absolute chagrin, one of the executives from my previous company joined my new company! I remember I was in the kitchen and literally fell to the floor when I read the announcement! He and I caught up soon after, and he said, 'I forgive you for what you did.'

This is a classic example of gaslighting and was definitely not a vindication for Pauline! This leader had no insight into the severity or consequentiality of the previous situation and no ownership of his complicity in siding with the previous

CEO at the time. However, Pauline soon learned that not all members of her last executive team members had the same reaction.

> *It was only years later, when I met one of my colleagues from that time, that I felt like I had done the right thing! One of the executives sadly lost his daughter to cancer about 10 years after all this happened. At that time, he wrote to the employee who had first approached me about the sexual harassment, 'All your allegations were right. I am so, so sorry I didn't do something about it and that I didn't help you at that time.'*

Many young women I speak with are surprised when I mention the prevalence of sexual harassment, bias and discrimination against women and marginalised groups at work today.

'Didn't we solve that in the seventies?' they'd ask.

And I'd say that I wish we had and that it was that simple.

In some ways, it is that simple. We must raise awareness of the blind spots we all have due to our inherent biases.[10] It's these biases that reinforce our stereotypical beliefs and allow behaviours to go unnoticed or unchallenged, especially when propagated by the most powerful people in the room.

Raising awareness is the responsibility of women too. Sharing stories about their current and past experiences helps others prepare to be on the lookout for those behaviours that don't feel or sit right in their gut. Like Pauline, who doubted whether she had done the right thing, many women feel the same way when confronted with sexual harassment and discrimination.

Jo: It takes time to recover from a bad manager

Jo McCatty is a recent Head of People & Culture, career strategist, podcast host and advocate for getting more women into STEM and leadership roles. After starting

---

[10] See Daniel Kahneman's Thinking, Fast and Slow

her career in science, she shifted to coaching because it fuels her passion for people. She loves to help people find their next perfect role and future, and in that work, she has helped many regain their confidence after negative workplace experiences. At times she has helped people in roles that lack the growth they need so they are looking for a new challenge: when they are ready, yet not quite confident.

Everyone's different, depending on their life circumstances and whatever they've been subjected to, especially in the work environment. I have found that if you've had a leader who isn't empowering and supporting you, it takes a lot longer to come back to yourself again and find that career confidence to 'start betting on yourself'.

Irrespective of gender, if the leader doesn't have the leadership skills to inspire, support and encourage, it can be so demoralising. They downplay, they micromanage, and they tell you how you're lacking in something rather than reinforcing the positive or coaching and guiding you to success. The tone they communicate with and the words they use are demeaning versus empowering. I don't want to use the word toxic because that could mean so many things, but it's like they see life through a negative lens, and that energy then spreads to their team.

I really don't like seeing people in that pain and suffering, and I have every intention of helping them along the way, but in their own timeline. The longer they've been subjected to it, the harder it is to overcome it. But once they do, it's amazing.

Melanie's big lessons

After years of career success in project management across various senior roles in diverse organisations, Melanie found herself bruised and feeling broken from an experience of a manager who micromanaged and broke her confidence. Melanie's story demonstrates the impact of the 'bad manager' experience and how working in a supportive environment turned things around for her.

I'm very thankful for that time in my life. I loved the people. I loved the culture and the environment. It gave me a lot. My team was great. Within a month of starting on a project that was in trouble, I had it turned around and we delivered successfully. It just needed some governance around it. It wasn't a big deal, but the executive sponsor, Michelle, became excited that I fixed it. She was super excited with my capability, and they kept giving me more projects. It was Michelle who sponsored me into the new permanent role of Senior Project Manager in Jean's team.

I quickly found that I had a very different style from my manager, Jean. My style is listening, obtaining information and bringing people on a journey to get to an outcome. Jean is all about the numbers and data and making sure that things are perfect. That caused friction because she felt that I was unprepared. Every day, and I'm not joking, I would hear, 'What you're doing is not exactly ready. I don't approve it.' From someone who came into the organisation and became a rock star, I was now getting my work corrected with a red pen.

We had a conversation, and I said, 'Jean, you have to stop micromanaging me. I can't do my job.'

'I don't have faith in your ability', she said.

We couldn't resolve it. Everyone on the floor, by this stage, knew that there was tension between us. My Director (Jean's boss), then, got involved. A couple of people had spoken to her about it.

The Director organised a meeting. I was excited because I wanted her help to resolve the relationship breakdown between Jean and myself. We met in a coffee shop at the bottom of the building. It's really relaxed. After some small talk, with a smile on her face, she changed the topic.

'I know what's going on with you and Jean. Do you not understand that she's your manager? You are the one that will lose your job.'

She ripped me apart for a good twenty minutes. I sat there and listened; she would not let me dispute any of the points, and she did it all with a smile. I have never seen anything like that in my entire career.

After that, Jean sent me a bunch of unachievable tasks, which I tried to accomplish. But at that stage, my confidence was shot. I had no support from my manager.

She told me multiple times that she had no faith in my capability and regretted hiring me. She actually said that!

'Well,' I said to her, 'if you do not stop, I will put a bullying claim against you. I'm going to HR. I can't take this anymore.'

After speaking to HR, I resigned. I went on a holiday with my family literally the next week. I decompressed for that week, then had a month off where I just walked and tried to understand and process what had happened.

Then, I started a new job that I was headhunted for. And, honestly, I had the most incredible managers there. It was just about delivering my outcomes. I loved the team and the organisation. I felt like I was doing something that was adding value.

In time, I told my new manager what had happened at my previous organisation. He listened; he was empathic. He said to me, 'We got you. I have no doubt that you're going to get back on your feet quickly. But right now, I'm going to give you stuff that's not too complicated that I know you'll be able to turn around in a heartbeat. What I want you to do is promise me that every day for an hour, you're going to get out and walk by the river. I want you to go for a walk and not think about this place. I want you to switch off.'

It was all about mental health. He could see that I wasn't in a great place then, so his response was to nurture and empower me.

So, anyway, I delivered my outcomes and got back on my feet quite quickly. I started to gain confidence, and then they gave me a very complex project to fix. It was over budget by $2 million, and I turned that around. Everyone was pleased.

I then got promoted and ran the project team again, which went successfully. Then they moved me to Operations to sort out their technical engineering, which I did. They got me to run the whole account. That was all in a period of four years.

I look back, and I can see that everything that happened to me taught me a lesson. Jean taught me a lesson. I know now that if you don't have the support you need in a particular role, you will not be successful. Jean taught me what not to do. Collaboration, empowerment and vulnerability are the best things a leader can provide to their group.

I'm now leading the senior team. I deal with very senior people who feel empowered to be their best versions at work. I give them the ability to make their own decisions about how they want to do things, but I'm also willing to listen, provide guidance and set boundaries to ensure and enable their success. For me, that's important as a leader. I'm not looking to push people down and take the credit. I very rarely take credit for myself.

Time and time again, I hear women talk about the adverse impacts of control and command leadership that Melanie experienced in her previous organisation. In my PhD research, I found that the lack of a nurturing culture had negative impacts on women's job satisfaction and career success more so than men's. I have no doubt that many men suffer in silence as well, putting up with environments devoid of nurturance and empathy, where dominance and competition is the standard leadership style.

Chapter 3

New Philosophy of Positive Femininity

☆ ☆ ☆ ☆ ☆

We can define a new philosophy for leading through positive femininity. Traditional models of femininity are passive and keep women subservient in roles no longer required in a complex and uncertain world.

Positive femininity describes gender identity as active characteristics of our personality that are expressive (in feeling) and positive masculinity as defined by more instrumental characteristics (in action).

Gender identity is fluid and separate from biological sex. However, due to cultural beliefs and our early socialisation, masculinity tends to be associated with men and femininity with women. We have built stereotypes and cultural taboos around behaviour contradictory to these traditional associations. In fact, people demonstrate both femininity and masculinity at any given time.

When stereotypical roles are imposed according to gender, this can be harmful in limiting opportunities for personal growth and careers. For women, the more passive gender role imposed on them is contrary to what is required in leadership roles. Often, women are regulated to mother, counsellor and seductress roles; rewarded for being passive and submissive; and admonished for being dominant, assertive and independent. These gender stereotypes start very early in life – from the childhood playground where girls are called 'bossy' when boys are called 'strong'. These stereotypes continue to play out in how we think about leadership roles as 'male' and in organisational cultures that are biased towards masculinity, competition and individualism over collaboration and communion.

We can define femininity more positively rather than give up on its utility for successful organisational life. Femininity comprises active traits associated with the skillset required in modern organisations, such as an awareness of feelings, nurturance, compassion and collaboration. We are seeing these capabilities gain traction in new leadership styles and as key cultural determinants. These capabilities are being singled out by organisations that value their staff and customers and believe that a more authentic and personal relationship is key to sustainable success.

Authors like Peter Senge and Brene Brown have raised awareness of the importance of creating healthier human systems in work, leadership and the planet. In Sweden, a group of key thought leaders have come together to accelerate the United Nations' global Sustainable Development Goals by advocating for Inner Development Goals, which include capabilities of Being (relationship to self), Thinking (cognitive skills), Relating (caring for others and the world), Collaborating (social skills) and Acting (driving change). Many of these capabilities require positive feminine characteristics that have been devalued in the workplace in the past but are now seen as vital to creating workplaces that are 'fit for humans'.

The wicked problems in the world today need the application of feminine attributes. We need collaboration and a different way of leading. We need another way of thinking about complex problems. To solve complex problems within an economy that is volatile, ambiguous and uncertain, we need to be networked. Social connection is more important than ever because we need all our collective voices and perspectives to think of new solutions and better ways to achieve them. We need positive femininity; the old masculine models don't serve us anymore.

Women are great connectors

Women tend to be great connectors. We learn this very early on, from infancy to our early years. We treat boys and girls differently from when they're babies. We hold a baby differently, depending on whether they are a boy or a girl. We demonstrate more nurturing, gentle behaviours towards a female infant, whereas people will usually apply a rough-and-tumble approach with a male infant.

In the incredibly malleable brain of the infant, this can lead to differences between boys and girls in their risk assessment. Boys learn that they can be safe even when thrown up into the air by their fathers, while girls are encouraged to stay nestled into their chests for protection.

In a study that dressed female infants in boys' clothing and male infants in girls' clothing, the female infants dressed as 'boys' were more often described as angry, whilst the female infants dressed as 'girls' were more often described as happy and social.[11] We are reinforcing an idea of connection and nurturance for female infants, which then forms our processing bias as adults.

When we see ourselves as part of our environment, we consider connection more. If I walk into an organisation where I see myself connected rather than separate from the environment, I'm more likely to look for connections; I'll prioritise relationships with others. I'm looking for ways in which those relationships are being enhanced or nurtured. I'll also look beyond the relationships of the people I see around me to the relationships of their relationships. So, there's a spider's web of relationships that I am sensitive to. I will look at my peers, clients and suppliers in that way. Therefore, I might see a solution through these connections.

In contrast, this solution may not become apparent if I have a perceptual bias towards seeing myself and others as separate and individualistic, which is often the case in corporations where individual competition is rewarded.

---

[11] Lise Eliot (2009). Pink brain, blue brain: how small differences grow into troublesome gaps-- and what we can do about it. Boston, Houghton Mifflin Harcourt.

Achieving balance between the view of myself as connected and the view of myself as an individual is a key motivating drive for evolving as human beings, according to Jungian Psychologist David Bakan.[12] Bakan believes that feminine traits or strengths create in women a self-identity that is connected and prioritises connection. The challenge for women, then, is to learn some characteristics related to differentiating themselves as independent from their environment. In development terms, this might be learning to speak up or becoming a leader differentiated from others. It's about overcoming the hesitancy of self-promotion (women often describe their achievements by saying *we* rather than *I*) and the desire to be liked.

This predisposition for connection is also a powerful strength. Marketers have known this for years. They know that people are more likely to trust a brand when they see it connecting with the causes consumers believe in. The positive femininity driver in us scans for things in our environment that reinforce our idea of connection and see the opportunity for connection to the larger environment that customers expect.

For example, the staff at Google formed a minority union of about 800 to collectively pressure the corporation to make decisions aligned to 'not creating evil in the world'.[13] They cared about aligning the organisation they worked for to the causes they cared about.

We also see a connection priority in the move towards digital transformation and agile ways of working, which requires engagement with more people so that we get diversity in ideas that drive innovation. Innovation requires you to start with and leverage connection for setting priorities and brainstorming solutions.

At this point, I want to remind you that I am referring to psychological gender and not biology. Not all women will be great connectors, and some men will be. Nevertheless, the strength they bring comes from a trait borne of positive femininity.

---

[12] D Bakan, Duality of Human Existence: Isolation and Communion in Western Man, Beacon Press, 1971.

[13] B Allyn, 'Google Workers Speak Out About Why They Formed A Union: "To Protect Ourselves"', NPR, 2021, https://www.npr.org/2021/01/08/954710407/at-google-hundreds-of-workers-formed-a-labor-union-why-to-protect-ourselves.

Psychological femininity is where our capability to connect, nurture and empathise comes from. Nurturance is showing someone that you care and are willing to empower and take their perspective because you understand that their success begets your success.

Care became a key value during the COVID-19 pandemic. It was one of those differentiators for organisational cultures and governments. It is not a coincidence that the female-led countries handled Covid better during the crisis. Think of the early success of leaders such as Germany's Angela Merkel, New Zealand's Jacinda Ardern, Denmark's Mette Frederiksen, Taiwan's Tsai Ing-wen and Finland's Sanna Marin. These countries locked down earlier and had fewer deaths compared to countries led by men.[14]

We can think about organisations as being structured in feminine and masculine terms as well. Organisations or institutions are structured so that people can differentiate themselves from their environment, often valuing agency over communion. The organisational culture will reward people for setting themselves apart from their environment, which drives competitive behaviours and aggressive modes of operation. Whilst competition is necessary for some industries where innovation is driven by different teams competing to be the first to solve a particular problem, aggressive competition leads to distrust, siloes and political muckraking in most organisations.

The future of work, and indeed the planet, requires capabilities that are grounded in trust, collaboration and connection. More and more organisations provide the structure for people to live their lives. They nurture well-being and sustainability through benefits like healthcare and superannuation. However, this is just the start. More and more employees are looking to organisations to provide an environment where they can thrive and flourish. If leaders want to build a culture of trust in their organisations, they need to show that in their hearts, they have the success of others as a priority along with the organisation. It's pretty simple.

I'm deliberately talking about the **heart**.

---

[14] J Henley, 'Female-led countries handled coronavirus better, study suggests', The Guardian, 2020, https://www.theguardian.com/world/2020/aug/18/female-led-countries-handled-coronavirus-better-study-jacinda-ardern-angela-merkel.

We often don't think about heart as being relevant to business, but care is how people connect on a real, deep level. As a leader, if I truly care about my staff and customers and want to help them succeed and achieve their dreams, then they will respond with loyalty and trust. And that's great for business!

Reconciling the different aspects of myself

How do we embrace our unique positive feminine strengths in both leadership and life? Firstly, we need to understand why these traits have been undervalued. Traditional forms of femininity have had significant adverse consequences because passive femininity has been attributed to women and traditional women's roles. It's caused incredible problems in work–life balance for women as they try to fulfil those traditional roles as well as other roles at work. We can see this evidenced in recent division of labour statistics.

Workplace Gender Equality Agency's 2020 research states, 'Globally, women perform 76.2% of the hours of unpaid care work, and men perform less than a quarter of the hours of unpaid care work.' Whilst the Covid pandemic has seen more men working from home, the average hours each week in unpaid care work is only 36.1%, whilst it's 64.4% for women.[15] This distribution has nothing to do with who is most capable or interested in these roles, but more about whom stereotypes dictate should be responsible for these roles. These attitudes limit women's opportunities to build confidence and capability in other areas of work and life and restrict their beliefs about the possibility of their potential.

In my twenties, I struggled with what kind of woman I wanted to be. I was doing my PhD, working part-time at the university and working as a professional belly dancer. I remember my supervisor at the time asking me, 'How do you reconcile your feminist values and your professional role with the fact that you belly dance?' At that time, belly dancing was more taboo than today, and I often hid that part of my life from my professional colleagues. I know now that the energy that went into compartmentalising my life in that way was futile and, in fact, had adverse

---

[15] 'Gendered Impact of COVID-19', Workplace Gender Equality Agency, 2020, https://www.wgea.gov.au/publications/gendered-impact-of-covid-19.

effects on my ability to truly connect with the people around me. They weren't getting the real me because I didn't bring my whole self to that workplace.

Traditional gender roles haven't worked for men, either. Men are equally locked into gender roles that place excessive focus on achieving at work at the expense of neglecting their relationships and family ties. Men want more meaningful, complex lives than the masculine stereotype currently allows for. Masculine forms of leadership have shown time and again, through decades of social research, not to work for creating productive teams and strong organisational cultures. It does not drive motivation, or productivity, or effectiveness. It does not drive profits for shareholders. It just does not work. So, we need a third way.

In my PhD research, I found that women could 'do masculinity' as effectively as men in the workplace. They were capable and confident in demonstrating both masculine and feminine characteristics in their leadership roles. Still, they suffered from the lack of nurturance and connection in their organisational cultures. When they described culture, they didn't see positive femininity reflected back at them. Instead, they saw passive femininity and hyper forms of masculinity such as ruthlessness, competition and aggressiveness. This had adverse impacts on their ability to thrive in their leadership roles. What we need is a new form of leadership that tilts more towards positive femininity than traditional masculinity. We need to focus on women's strengths and stop apologising for them.

What if our workplace and societal cultures were more focussed on values of connectedness, a world of peace and beauty, family security, forgiveness, inner harmony, self-respect, true friendship, honesty and nurturing ways to relate to each other and our customers? These are the things that positive femininity brings us. How can we create environments that embody those positive feminine attributes? How do we unleash, grow and keep our power?

Chapter 4

Playing to Your Unique Feminine Strengths

☆ ☆ ☆ ☆ ☆

'She was lavish. She was a dark, unyielding largess. She was, in short, too bloody much ...' Richard Burton on Elizabeth Taylor

Stop doubting your gut. Develop a personal brand that is closer to your authentic self. Don't apologise for being different. Remember, the world needs you and your unique strengths.

In my career, on many occasions, I was told that I was a square peg in a round hole – too emotional, too colourful, too different. I worked with a coach, hoping to hone those characteristics that would make me a better fit for leadership. Through that deep work, I discovered there was nothing wrong with me. What my bosses referred to as derailers were, in fact, strengths. The truth of the matter was that I was beautifully round – it was the hole that was square!

Tina's journey out of a square hole

Tina has a degree in Engineering and has enjoyed a successful career in Business Improvement, working with companies undergoing transformation. She is intelligent, insightful and passionate about people. Early on, she thought that her career plan was clearly laid out in front of her. She was progressing successfully through every step, until one day she realised the road she was on was someone else's path.

As a young person, I believed that I had a responsibility to take on the family business, which was an engineering-based business. That wasn't based on anything anyone told me or even suggested, but it was an unsaid expectation.

On the weekends, I used to go to my dad's factory. Looking around, I'd see a world I felt I needed to be responsible for. I chose to do engineering, but part way through my degree, I had a breakdown. I had a flashback of myself at about the age of 12, standing in that factory, making a pact in my mind that I would need to take over the family business. I had buried that memory. It was a tough time of my life.

Three-quarters of the way through the degree, I thought, Why am I doing engineering? Why am I here? I don't even know if this is what I want to be.

I did manage to finish the degree, and then I went on a period of self-searching through that time. I was working part-time because of the nature of the degree. I started exploring other options. I saw a life coach, and that was an amazing experience. I only saw her three times, but the process she took me through was listing out all the things I love doing, listing all the things I know I'm good at and then looking for synergies between the two.

That process helped me stop looking at myself as an Engineer but as a person with strengths and skills and passions. Working through my breakdown helped me decide what direction to take myself into without pigeonholing myself by what I studied.

I now work in a heavily engineering-dominated industry with more males than females. I found myself fighting it for a while, and then I learnt to lean into it and not be afraid of my environment. I run change transformation-type projects, and I bring that human face to what is quite often seen as just a very tactical project. This has resonated quite well in the many challenging initiatives I've been involved with. Right now, I don't think I could do a project without bringing the human face or EQ side into it, so I absolutely do believe that I use it every day.

Where I work is incredibly innovative. They develop some pretty amazing technologies. But at the end of the day, if you don't take the people on the journey, you just don't end up with good outcomes. If you engage people not only with their minds but with their hearts and passions, you bring that alignment upfront and get far better outcomes. It blows my mind.

I did my thesis on this when I was at university. I researched how we improve the efficiency of manufacturing. When I look back at my thesis, it was predominantly about engaging stakeholders early on. So even as a young researcher, I knew the importance of truly connecting with the people.

Gwen discovers that diversity is a superpower

After feeling conflicted about her mixed racial identity and challenging the gender identities playing out after becoming a partner in her firm, Gwen discovered that her perceived weaknesses in one context could be regarded as unique strengths in another.

I didn't want to be treated differently, which has been a struggle my whole life. In Hong Kong, I always said hello in Chinese even though everybody said hi. *I felt like I had to constantly prove to everybody that I was one of them.*

I didn't realise, until I worked in New York City, that being different was like my superpower. People would ask me, 'Where's your accent from?' I look Chinese but speak with a slight English accent.

For once, being from multiple cultures wasn't something I was trying to hide. It was seen as a bonus that I brought to the table. I had never felt like that before, and it was so liberating. That totally changed how I saw the whole world. I thought,

Here is a world where people are used to dealing with people coming from different perspectives, and it's a good thing rather than a deficit.

It brought back a memory of when I was at school, and my history teacher, who had taught me for six years by this point, said, 'Gwen, you can ask for special consideration because English is not your first language.'

I was really offended because, in my mind, my English was perfectly fine!

Learning more about women's empowerment and gender equality in the last decade also liberated me. I am more sure about my own gender identity being a superpower as well. I remember sitting with some male colleagues in Hong Kong, whom I had known for many years, and listening to these guys talk about female colleagues in a derogatory way. I was quite offended, really disgusted.

Previously, I probably would have sat there and thought, Oh, they're just boys being boys. *But for the first time, I looked at it differently. The women they were discussing were colleagues in my team, and there was a strong sense in my mind that this was not right, and so I voiced that.*

They looked at me, as if asking, 'What is wrong with you?'

'Seriously, this is not okay," I said.

Since then, I haven't had dinner with them again.

Rachel: My creative intuitive superpower

Rachel has always known that creativity and intuition were her superpowers, yet her story is about how she is still second-guessing.

My mom had three children under 3 years old, and I was in between my two brothers. I didn't get a lot of attention as a kid, but I never really was an attention seeker. I spent a lot of time alone growing up because my brothers would play together. I often just went off on my own, thinking and creating.

I was very creative. I was in touch with my creative side and intuition, which is absolutely a strength of women. Our power comes from knowing how to be in touch with it and listen to it.

However, as I've gotten older – and I think I am still doing this – I second-guess it. I think that develops from a very young age as a female unless it's squashed. It comes from a very deep place. As girls and women, we can see and have foresight, but it's not necessarily taken seriously or valued. Men have intuition as well, of course. But as the historically dominant sex, they've always been listened to and valued for their opinions, whereas women's opinions are less valued in a lot of ways.

As I've grown older I've realised there is definitely a need for men to be more in touch with their feminine side too. Having coached several men most recently to help them overcome self-doubt, I realise – through their stories of being squashed from an early age, usually by their fathers – that the process is similar for men. If only we knew how to be more in touch with our feminine side, how to balance the feminine and masculine and our superpowers, people across the world would be in a much better position to be healed.

Olivia's approach to leadership in a world that can't stop talking

Olivia is in her twenties and the early stages of her career as a Psycholologist. She is discovering how to use her unique strengths in the leadership roles she's aspiring to. She is just about to recruit her first staff member and is looking forward to doing leadership her way.

I've been reading a book called Quiet Power: The Secret Strengths of Introverts by Susan Cain. It's about the power we all bring to leading – whether female or male, introverted or extroverted. It also speaks to how you can influence in different ways. For so long, there's been a stereotypical view of a leader as male, dominant and directing. That's not really who I am. I guess, getting some leadership training had quite a significant impact for me. I saw how you can be so effective in a broader, gentler and more emotional way. It's about applying emotional intelligence and empowering people.

I feel lucky when I think about the people I've worked for, having had great leaders along the way. I've been thinking about the kind of leader I want to be. I've seen what's worked well in the past, and I'm now emulating that in my own leadership style. An approach I'd like to hopefully take on myself is one from my current manager. He is such a good leader with a good balance between being empowering and giving free rein to just run with things. He's very supportive and very much there when you need to talk and get guidance and direction.

Something that also really resonates with me is that approach of empowering and taking a real team or partnership approach. In my last role, my manager's style was forming a partnership. Everything was open – there were no secrets, no hierarchy. We all pulled together as one and worked as one. She absolutely reframed leadership for me because it differed from that hierarchical approach I was used to seeing.

The other important qualities I want to bring to leadership are being able to work with a team, supporting people in their development goals and driving innovation. I love the kind of leadership where you can be empowering and really bring about change in new ideas through encouraging diversity of thought. Also, just being able to have more of an impact, having more of a seat at the table and being able to contribute in a more impactful way – that appeals to me.

Lucia: Nurturing energy

With over 10 years of experience, and only in her late twenties, Lucia is the founder of Zelesco Consulting, a digital agency with a vision to work with disruptive game changers of the world and empower business owners to stand out as leaders in their niche. Early on, she displayed a drive for excellence in digital marketing and has always believed in learning on the job. She never took no for an answer, even when others told her she wouldn't make it or didn't know enough to get started. For Lucia, power is an individual spiritual force that is awakening in women right now.

I really believe in action and that you create your reality. From a young age I knew I would be a leader, and I chose business as my platform. I had six internships, all unpaid, when I was about 19. From there, I got all my clients and started selling.

I loved interacting with people. It was fun, and it was positive. I would get these visions and follow the feeling of happiness. I enjoyed the marketing world. I didn't know how I would do it, but I threw myself into running an agency. I knew straight up that I've got to work hard and that I should go in that direction.

What I am seeing, what is popping up more, is that more women are stepping forward. Women now are qualified and smarter but, unfortunately, still about 90% of them lack confidence. That's because men try to squash them down. Not only that, but women are also jealous of other successful women. But there is a spiritual awakening and a shift in the energy happening right now, and it's starting with feminine energy in the world.

When you take the time to work on yourself, you can realise that the power and gifts are inside you. You can realise that you can be who you want to be – your authentic self. It's often through the hardships and the pain that you realise that was your gift.

In my family, I was put down so much. It was a gift to realise that they were making me so strong because business is hard. I went from a place where it was really negative to forcing myself into the positive. Those pains you go through, you need to be able to weather them. Everybody has that power trapped inside of themselves. It's just about doing the work, getting with the right people and shining.

During the industrial revolution, we created machines and technology – that's male-dominated energy. Now we're going back to the spiritual, maternal, nurturing energy again – our spiritual awakening. Now things are changing, and the shift is coming, so men are just scared. We are now seeing a big shift to businesses putting people before profit. There are companies that are really thriving, caring about the planet, their community, and having a wider vision and mission to make a change. This is a more holistic approach to business that is very successful today.

Women are stepping forward as leaders in these forums and platforms. They are guiding the world to a better place. On every second house, during the recent federal government election campaign, there were women on all the billboards. I've never seen that before. I have never seen that in all the elections I've experienced. I saw woman after woman on the houses, and I'm so glad it's happening.

Ilona's values compass

For Ilona, a seasoned HR Executive Consultant, superpower came in the way of empathy and compassion in leadership. With more than 25 years of experience in human resources, transformation and change, she is the CEO and Co-Founder of Shilo People.

I came up through employer relations, dealing with employees and unions. To be successful in that role, you have to have a great deal of empathy for each of those parties. The goal is to get an outcome – the best outcome for everybody. I had a particularly pragmatic approach to dealing with employee relations, and it wasn't to get rid of unions at all costs.

Often, there were conversations I would find infuriating because we'd be going over the same old things. It felt like we'd go around in circles. I would sit and listen for a period. I couldn't get a word in for a long time, and then I'd suddenly just blurt out whatever it was I'd been storing up. It would just come out really, very strongly. It would stop the whole conversation, which was not very good. I did get a bit of feedback that I was always that black hat, always putting a different point of view forward. I think there is value in not being the only one doing that, as that can have a negative impact personally. But for me, it came from a place of empathy.

Throughout those early years, I got noticed and promoted. I still don't know exactly why. I think I'm good at what I do – I'm very efficient and do what I say I'm going to do. From an integrity point of view, I think that's really important. Generally, the feedback I received was that I delivered excellent outcomes. Even in my junior days, I would be super efficient and get the work done. From a technical delivery perspective, I think that certainly helps earlier in your career.

As I took on more leadership roles, I got a lot of feedback that my leadership style suits many people. I think I'm what you would hope a good leader is. I believe in giving people autonomy to do their jobs. I feel passionate about developing and pushing them beyond what they think they can do and giving them the opportunities to do that. I would have great teams because I attracted some amazing people who were so good.

Rebecca: Vulnerability is key

Rebecca is a Salesforce MVP, Product Owner and proud Woman in Technology. As well as being Head of Business Systems Success at QIC Real Estate, she is also a powerlifter and strongwoman, having represented Australia twice on international competitions.

Rebecca, like Ilona, is a compassionate leader who believes in the unique power she brings to her leadership role, particularly in tough times. Authentic in her leadership style, Rebecca raised herself to positions by garnering the power of trust and empathy.

I'd been a manager in lots of different positions, but I didn't really step into my power until I started working at a financial services organisation. We had national contracts with some small organisations, and our contract meant a lot to them. I had to work with them and sometimes stop working with them, and so I learned that the power of my communication with other people comes from my positional power.

I remember the first time I had to cancel a national contract with a company that relied on us as one of their biggest customers. I had to call them and have the conversation – and conversations like that can go very badly or very well. You can do it by just sending people a letter and saying, 'You're cancelled', or you can take the time to step up and say, 'I'm going to have a compassionate and empathic discussion with this organisation, knowing that this is going to hurt them a lot', and try to make sure they understand the reasons why we are making that decision. I still remember that phone call. It helped me to shape future phone conversations from then on.

That's when I discovered my power of communication and how I was able to make sure that a very difficult phone call can still have a positive outcome. That helped me shape future phone calls and conversations I had. I learned about my empathy, decision-making and authentic behaviours from dealing with so many people in hiring and firing situations.

Working in a fast-paced environment, there was no time to be inauthentic or build a façade. There I learned vulnerability, because having to let someone go when you downsize is about having those hard conversations. Those are all the things that I think helped me build who I am today. I learned a lot of those things early, but I also look at them as tools in my tool belt. That makes me a better leader.

It's only been in the last two years of my career that I've started to see myself as a leader rather than a manager, and there's a huge difference between those roles. You can be a manager and not a leader, as far as I'm concerned. I'm a leader and have a leadership shadow that people can see, they can understand who I am and know what I stand for and what my values are.

People say that they're authentic leaders, that they're being their true selves, but they don't always live that fact. But I really do think I have authentic leadership. I'm able to gain trust from people and earn their respect, even though I speak very matter-of-factly. I don't beat around the bush. I'm also very honest and quick to apologise and be vulnerable. I make sure people understand that I'm not always right. If I am wrong, I will admit it and say, 'It's my fault this thing happened. How are we going to work to fix it?' I'm very much an open book. Really, I run my own style at work.

We work in a financial service organisation where people come to work with suits and ties – that's cool for them. But I've gone through every colour of hair in the rainbow. I'd recently changed my hair colour to pastel pink, and it coincided with the new Managing Director starting. I was in a meeting with him; he noticed and said, 'I love your hair.'

It's important to be your true self at work because that builds trust with people. That's why people respect you.

Vulnerability is key. If you're always just a wall, then you won't last very long.

Rebecca was able to curate a leadership style in a traditional financial workplace culture that was ready for change. However, not all are. In some organisations, deviating from the expected norms of leadership is risky. Many workplace cultures are based on masculine forms of power and influence, which rely on power over others rather than power **with** others. Therefore, independence and competition are prioritised over empathy and compassion, even though these traits may be valued.

Without a template for leadership and power, women mimic the forms of power we see expressed by those in influential positions before us. We adapt our styles to being 'square' rather than creating our uniquely feminine shapes through our leadership stye.

Pauline comes into her true feminine power

Pauline recently fulfilled a lifelong ambition and became CEO. She speaks about how it feels to finally be there and how she is deviating from expected leadership norms in the wider multinational organisation she works for.

> *It feels great, but it's been hard. Throughout these years, I've had to work out how to do it {leadership} and what I feel comfortable doing. I remember going through my career where I needed to present more as passively feminine, with my hair up all the time {Pauline has flowing, long curly hair and wears glasses} It messes with you. I dressed like that for quite a long time.*
>
> *When I started my career, it was a male-dominated industry. There weren't any women around, so I felt like that's what I needed to do. I was in the spotlight; people listened to me. But if I wanted people to do something, I felt like I needed to do it in a very soft way. Whereas the men were more upfront about their requests and demands, I took a more caring approach. The guys would just demand stuff.*
>
> *Then, I went through a phase of 'I'm just going to be me'. I'm not going to put my hair up anymore. I took my glasses off and started wearing contact lenses. I felt like I'd been hiding behind these glasses, so I became more me. I started wearing dresses rather than suits or combining both. I started coming out and being bolder in my clothing. It was only once I made this shift that I started to fly. What came*

next was more of who I was, more of my positive femininity and uniqueness. The more I became my authentic self, the better my results were and the career opportunities presented themselves to me.

Chapter 5

Letting Go of Old 'Power' Beliefs

☆ ☆ ☆ ☆ ☆

For many of the women in this book, their journey to power often included letting go of old beliefs about power that were holding them back in some way from fulfilling their true potential. We all have these beliefs. They are ingrained in us from a very early age in the societal cultures we grew up in. But as you'll see from the stories presented here, beliefs can change.

Nicole, on shifting power

Chinese-born Nicole, tells a story of how she shifted that power base within her by changing her enviornment. Nicole's early family experiences in China reinforced the marginal positions of women. Her father was untraditional in terms of expectations for his daughters but traditional in other ways about his role as the patriarch. Early experiences in her life reinforced her marginalisation within her family and culture.

I was shocked when I first came to Australia. I was probably seven or six. I came on my own to be with my grandmother. I remember coming off the plane and looking around, and thinking, Whoa, something's wrong.

The people sweeping the floor and serving at the counters – they were all white.

I thought, Where is everyone? Have they killed them or something?

My grandmother was the only Chinese person I could see. When she came out of the crowd at the airport, I was so relieved to see her because I thought I had been left in this white world that no one had told me about. I think sometimes I was pretty mad and traumatised by that because I came on my own. Yes, I was with my grandmother, but everyone around her were White Australians. Sometimes if I'm in a room full of white people, all of whom are probably on the same level as me, I can't say anything. I feel invisible.

I noticed that White people seem to be very free with their opinions and, at times, for some reason I feel I don't have one. I haven't got anything to say, or nobody wants to listen to it.

Today, Nicole is an award-winning film-maker. Her acclaimed documentary, Putuparri and the Rainmakers[16], tells a story about about the courage of Putuparri Tom Lawford, a Kimberley Wangkajunga man whose determined love of family, culture and traditional lands takes him on a hard yet profoundly rewarding journey all the way back to his desert home. Along the way Nicole learned about power through her connection with Putuparri's family.

I've had a lot of different and empowering experiences. When I was going back and forth to New York, I was very powerful. I just fell into film-producing and did huge jobs there. I was very confident about what I was doing. I did it very well and thought I would never leave New York. When I came to Australia, and no one knew me, I then descended into disempowerment. I questioned, 'Who am I?'

---

[16] PUTUPARRI AND THE RAINMAKERS is a feature length documentary that had its world premiere at the Melbourne International Film Festival followed by an international premiere at the Hotdocs Film Festival. It has been nominated for many awards and won Best Film at the 2015 CinefestOz Film Festival. (See https://putuparri.com/about-nicole-ma/)

LETTING GO OF OLD 'POWER' BELIEFS

I came back to Australia because my grandmother was dying. I hadn't been there for 13 years, and I didn't want her to die without me seeing her. It wasn't like I had thought it through. Yes, I had this huge career in New York. I thought I'll just go home for a year.

Well, she didn't die. So, I went to the Victorian College of the Arts and did a postgraduate degree. I had to do it, so I didn't just sit around while she was dying. She died that year. After that, friends in New York told me about this job at the National Museum in Australia. This was in 2000. I knew nothing about Australia. I felt a bit like a fraud. They had invited me to do it only because I was the only Australian they knew.

I said, 'I've never done anything like that. I've done films, but I've never done multimedia'.

'Okay, we'll just talk you through it,' they said.

So, I thought, Okay, I had that New York experience, and I could do this too.

When I got there, I found that half the museum was Aboriginal. What does that even mean? The Director was Aboriginal as well. I was fascinated.

I travelled all around Australia and met many different groups to place their art and decide what stories we would include in the National Museum of Australia. That's when I met Spider and Dolly (Putuparri's grandparents – Wirrali activist and artist Nyilpirr Ngalyaku 'Spider' Snell and Dolly Juguja Snell).

I was going to these remote communities and, at the same time, I was making this other film called Dances of Ecstasy. I thought I'll just ask them about ecstatic dance, seeing as I'm there. And they just laughed. They wanted me to do a film about Putuparri instead. I went into the desert with them. I'm an urban gal – I mean, I don't even go camping. I didn't like the outdoors. But we started going into the desert in Western Australia, and it was a spiritual realm. It was totally like nothing I had ever seen before. It was transformational for me – being with these people as we went further and further into the desert.

It took nearly a week to get there. Sometimes we would progress only about 10 kilometres a day. We didn't have cell service; we didn't have mirrors. We didn't have the structures where we look at ourselves all the time. I realised out there that I felt completely myself. I felt proud, and I felt beautiful. I felt with these people that I could just be who I was.

That was a totally new experience for me. I had never felt like that before. I was always either fighting for my identity or fighting for jobs, trying to prove myself. Out there, there was nothing to prove. We just had to survive. The focus was on water and food.

It was so transformative to sit in a space where I didn't judge myself. In my culture, there are times when, as an Asian woman, I feel small and no one sees me and I haven't got any boundaries. I'm too scared to speak up. But the way they treated me in the desert, there was no racism or gender at all. It was all very respectful, and everyone could be themselves. Now in our society, we call that being authentic. You're not left with yourself, where the critical side of yourself runs the show. Without mirrors and social media, you're not comparing yourself to anyone. That's all taken away.

It was a time when I reflected on when I felt disempowered. A lot of times, when I had successes, I never really believed I had the success. I'd think that it's for everyone else who had collaborated with me, and I just happen to be there. It's so strange; it's like a sense of denial of what you can and can't do. It's so very negative and stops you from accepting your magnificence.

Nicole remembers how meeting Dolly and Spider during the making of Putuparri fortified her sense of self and self-confidence.

The movie won an award with a $100,000 cash prize. It gave the film a huge spotlight. But it wasn't even winning the prize. By that stage, because of my experiences with Dolly and Spider, I felt them talking through me. I was able to channel them. When I first went into that room with all the white people, I just focussed on Dolly and Spider, then people became interested in the film. They were actually interested enough to come and see it, and they wanted to know what had really happened. They wanted to ask questions. So, I would say I'm just talking for the community.

Imposter syndrome in a world biased towards over-confidence

Right now, we see a bias towards extroversion and confidence in the workplace and on social media. In fact, both environments reward overconfidence regardless of a person's actual abilities.

There is power in confidence. However, current conceptions are individualistic and focus on win–lose outcomes. What would a more collective approach to power and confidence look like? What does confidence look like when we are focussed on co-creating power with others rather than power over others? How do we redefine our own sense of confidence so that we can tap into and unleash that source of power?

Olivia works through her negative self-talk

In her early career, Olivia struggled with self talk about being good enough. Luckily, she has an in-house mentor: her mum!

> *I'm really close with my mum, and she's always been so supportive. She encourages me – even with a people leader role when I saw it come up at work. It was a big step up from my last role. I wasn't sure if I'd be able to do it. She said, 'Just do it. You've got nothing to lose.'*
> *So, I went for it, and it ended up totally fine. But I definitely had that imposter syndrome.*

Olivia did get that role and is flourishing as a people leader, using values of empowerment as a leadership template with her team. She enjoys bringing positivity and fun to her team and focus on bringing the best out of her people. Olivia describes how she built confidence by developing competence in her new leadership role.

> *I drive a culture of information-sharing and innovation, and try to encourage the team to support each other and step in. I'm also mindful of creating psychological safety and encouraging them to speak up when they're not sure of something and*

have the confidence to bounce ideas off each other and challenge each other. As I step into the leadership role, it's solidifying those values for me that they do work to create a great team.

I'm getting positive feedback from others now that my team members enjoy coming to work and really want to be part of the team. When you get that feedback, you realise what you're doing is actually working. It's so great. I've really enjoyed it. I've really loved the people aspect of leadership.

What's been great is that the team is performing well in producing really good outcomes. When you get recognition from your peers and other leaders as well, it's so encouraging. It makes me think, Well, I am suited to this.

My negative self-talk has definitely reduced now that I'm formally in a leadership role. My confidence has increased as I've stepped into the leadership role and received feedback about what works.

Olivia's experience is a clear example of how competence builds confidence. You need the confidence to get started, then you build competence, which in turn builds more confidence. It's a self-fulfilling prophecy. In this context, Olivia's advice to other young women is both wise and insightful.

A really good piece of advice I heard is to start before you necessarily feel ready to. Rather than waiting until you feel like you have all the experience and qualifications and tick every box, just start doing it.

I asked Olivia if her mum was proud of her.

Yes, she is. She's still so supportive and so excited for me.

Rebecca: A woman in technology

Rebecca is a leader in her IT community, having achieved global recognition from the company that creates the software she works with every day, Salesforce. She is active within the Salesforce community and is often sought after for her help and advice and to create new connections. Despite her career success, she struggled with the feeling that somehow she was a fraud.

I didn't technically work in IT. No one called me a 'woman in technology'; it was a self-imposed label. I had a belief that I really wasn't a woman in technology and that I was faking it. There were other thoughts that I was going to be found out and that I didn't know enough about the technology I was using. The fear was that they were going to take the label from me.

After a while, I moved into a more senior role, leading a high-profile project for the business. The company was commencing a digital transformation project, which I put my hand up for. I wanted to be involved in the project because I knew it would transform the way our business worked every day. I also had some Background in using the Salesforce platform. In 2014, I implemented Salesforce with a small sales team. During this time I taught myself a lot about the platform, so I felt confident that I could support the business through this transformation.

I've become a well-known person in the Salesforce community. It's unlike any other technology ecosystem they've created. All these people who are administrators or developers, and even the end users on the customers' end of the platform, can go and ask each other how to do things, and everyone helps. In 2022 I was included in the annual Salesforce MVP cohort, which recognises high-level support and participation in the Salesforce community. And so, when this digital transformation program came up, I said, 'I'm the person for you. I'm the person that knows the platform that will be able to get people excited about using it.'

I gained confidence because of the external recognition. But then, actually working internally and showing people that this is why I had received the external recognition was a turning point. People were saying, 'Oh, it's about time you are being recognised for your expertise; we've always known you are a star.'

My response was, 'Well, it's nice to hear that because I haven't been told that very much before!'

But perhaps they didn't feel the need to verbalise it to me because I had been there for such a long time. I just built this respect and trust with everyone I work with in my part of the organisation.

'We already knew you were a leader; we already knew you were good,' they said.

It was probably me not hearing that and not being able to shake the shackles of imposter syndrome off.

I became more convinced when my organisation started investing in me as a leader. They sent me on an internal leadership program. It included an immersive offsite that gave me an opportunity to understand my leadership style and how to be an authentic leader. That also helped me unravel all those things and understand who I am, my values and what I bring to the organisation and my life in general.

I'd always thought of myself as an imposter; that others were putting me in lights, but they shouldn't because I'm sure there are plenty of other people who do the same thing as me and more. But when Salesforce – this global company that's worth billions of dollars – recognised me as a great advocate in the community, I also started recognising that status in myself and breaking through those shackles and saying, 'You're not an imposter. You've been recognised for a reason. You're good at what you do.' I really just started to believe in, respect and trust myself more. That was how I stepped into and believed I was a leader and not just an imposter.

From then on, it was just nice to back myself. I felt relief when I realised I didn't have to give these self-imposed beliefs any more oxygen. I felt relief that I'm not an imposter.

Cindy: Stepping into power after cancer

For Cindy, old beliefs were only shed after a second cancer diagnosis, as if the first wasn't enough!

The second time I was diagnosed with cancer, I was in a relationship. We were to get married in six weeks. I was in a very supportive relationship with a man who had my back. My then fiancé, Chris, said, 'Hey, I think you should actually down tools, park your business for a while, take the treatment you need.'

I needed chemo, and I really don't know how anyone would work and do that. You just feel so sick. Fortunately, I was in a very different situation personally, which afforded me the luxury of stopping work and putting the focus on myself.

Chris and I had this conversation very early in the piece. He said, 'Cindy, you have a lot of people who love you, and they want to support you, so let them in.'

One of the massive things I did differently was to be vulnerable and let people in, let people see me wherever I was falling apart, bald, ugly, sad, crying, whatever. I just thought, warts and all, you're getting it. I'm not sugar-coating this. People did support me, and that surprised me – how much people wanted to support me and how much they did support me because I let them in.

Vulnerability is something that I had always equated with weakness and dependence. Those words scared me. But for us to heal, we need to express our truth and connect with others. We need to feel safe to be seen just as we are. You can't do that when you're shut down. So, I started a podcast. I'm having those conversations that are a little bit scary. One woman I interviewed lost her mother to cancer. We talked about her grief and how she made peace with that and how she supported her mum through that.

During all that, I've had a massive shift in identity – if cancer doesn't do that to you, I don't know what would. I had thrown everything in the air and asked, 'Who am I now? What do I want to do with the rest of my life? What's most important to me? What do I value?'

What having cancer the second time meant for me was work. This time it was inner work. It has completely shifted my direction. Everything I've done in my career to date has prepared me for now. And I'm now working completely differently: I've written a book, which is such a beautiful piece of work and a passion project and something I'm super proud of. I have a range of cancer gifts and hampers. I have a free meditation series that people can get and I am doing a little bit of coaching work. I'm working in a space of helping.

I'm still in the process of reinventing myself post-cancer, but I see two linked sides. One side is helping people on their cancer journey, whether it's a diagnosis and treatment or beyond. I help them navigate from a psychological and emotional perspective with greater ease and grace. The other side, which is showing up for me, is working with high-performing women to help them have more balance.

I now want to work with people because I see so many anxious, exhausted and overwhelmed women. I work with high-performing women so that they can be more sustainable and balanced within themselves to perform at that level but in a sustainable, more human way.

It's a similar story to the one I told myself: I'm not enough. I need to keep striving. I need to keep producing to be valued and worthy. I need to fill in as much in my day, week and month and life as I possibly can. There's no time to rest. There's no time to be. It's all about doing.

They tell themselves: I've got so much to do, I'm so busy, and I'm so important.

But it's such a myth, a fallacy. That's the pattern I see. If only you could see that you are enough just as you are. There's no race to the end. You don't have to fill in as much as you can in life.

One of the meditations I do, which is one of my favourites, is meeting your future self 20 years from now, gleaning her insights and wisdom and bringing that back to now. That was such an aha, I thought, I am enough. I've already done enough. Anything is right, and I don't have anything to prove. I am who I am.

I recently saw this author – I bought her book and followed her on Instagram. In one of her posts, she's out on some yacht with her family, and I thought, Are book sales that great? How is she doing that? Why aren't I on a yacht? What does it say about me?

Comparison set in. I thought to myself, What she is doing and projecting into the world is her journey and actually says nothing about me. I refuse to let my thoughts head in that direction these days. You are enough already. There's no race. Nature doesn't hurry, and everything is accomplished.

I want to enjoy the journey a bit more and allow myself to stop and smell the roses rather than race through. I'm still challenged by that, however. I wouldn't say I've landed it yet because I still like that adrenaline. I like to get stuff done, and I like crossing stuff off my list. That's just who I am. It's because I learned very young in life to put on a façade, and I was rewarded for doing so. As the eldest child, I was encouraged and applauded for being strong, for being independent, for achieving. My parents wanted me to be a good role model. I learned I had to keep showing up that way to be strong and self-reliant. That was what I was rewarded for.

Jo: Find your superpowers

Jo talks about the beliefs that drive us to see leadership through a masculine lens, which drives in women a continual need to prove themselves as the 'outsider'.

The key starting point is that in society, we think through the lens of a man. When it comes to the work environment, women must elbow their way through. It's happening less and less, but we still must do it.

We are seen differently in the work environment when we're being assertive or speaking up. We're seen as aggressive as opposed to males. It's the male lens that makes women start to think they need to behave like men in leadership. I think it's now starting to shift with more awareness that in fact you need to be yourself. You need to have that self-confidence and speak up. That's why you need to see more and more women doing it, so you feel like you can also give yourself permission.

Women always have to prove themselves when they are not given opportunities or are overlooked and not tapped on the shoulder to say, 'I think you're capable of doing this.'

I have seen a theme of women coming to me saying, 'I've been in the business for a long time, Jo, and I have to find my way to my next role. There was an opportunity that came up, and I wasn't asked the question, "Would you be interested in exploring this?"'

Rightly or wrongly, maybe there is a reason behind it. But we need to be more conscious about women's career pathways and internal mobility. What females do in all the roles they fulfil in work and life are transferable to new roles. However, those transferable skills may not be apparent at first. So as leaders and recruiters, we need to be on the lookout for those transferable skills and do that more consciously.

The career coaching program I created is for men as well as women. It caters to everyone, depending on how they see themselves. The first step, before you make any change in your career or life, is self-evaluation.

We often bumble along when it comes to our careers. But if we sit there and consciously think about it and do an assessment, a self-evaluation, we figure out what our skills are and what we love doing.

I encourage my clients to think about past achievements: What are the things you're most proud of? What are the things that defined you? Some of them are about adversities and overcoming them. What are the big decisions and choices you've made? Then start to frame yourself according to what your superpowers are.

Being able to articulate your professional story in a way where you come across as self-confident and aware of your skills means you're not second-guessing yourself. I'm not saying you're completely perfect. You always want to learn and grow, but the starting point is: Don't be afraid to share. You can share your achievements and not feel shy about them. Be proud of that because it will enable you to open doors for yourself and others.

Self-evaluation is key. That's the advice I give to anyone I'm coaching, who's embarking on a new change.

It's the sense of empowering self. It's putting yourself first and not making a comparison to others. Being inspired by others but not comparing yourself to them. Don't say, 'I'm lacking what they've got. I'm not like that, but I want to be.'

Instead, say, 'No, I want to be myself and inspire and be inspired.'

Pauline's words of wisdom: Stay bold, stay curious

Be bold. Be absolutely bold. Don't feel that you must be this intelligent person with all the answers or the smartest person in the room. It's okay to ask questions. You'll probably end up being the smartest person in the room at the end of the day because you're the one asking the questions.

Young women are hungry at this point. But it's not just young women; it's men as well. They're ambitious and want to climb the corporate ladder quickly. They are focussed on their next move.

Stop always looking for that next move. Don't rush it, and don't have this urgency about it because that comes off as negative as well. People will see your strength and your power. When the right opportunity comes, you'll be ready to put your hand up for it or people will tap you on the shoulder and the doors will open.

Elissa: Staying pretty, beautiful, glamourous and sexy

Elissa is beautiful, in her 40s with long blonde hair and a poised and graceful presence about her. She is driven and ambitious and has navigated her career and personal life using masculine and feminine sources of power. Her story talks about how women use their sexual power through both lenses.

> *It's very much part of the gender role, isn't it, to be pretty and beautiful and glamorous? The type of power some women rely on is so much about wielding sexuality. It will attract in a man's objectification. I learned there are consequences for the woman herself in using that kind of power.*
>
> *I got into a relationship with a very charismatic guy who made me feel like I was beautiful, like a goddess. I felt like I was powerful. But I only felt powerful when he was telling me that I was beautiful. When he wasn't there, I would feel bad about myself. So, I would try to make myself more sexual.*
>
> *Eventually, after some time, he told me he wanted to open the relationship and make it polyamorous. But that was not real. He just wanted to be exposed to more*

sexual partners regardless of how I felt. I just went along with that. I accepted that, even though it was excruciating and terribly traumatising for me. He kept telling me something was wrong with me because I wasn't open enough. I felt inadequate and insecure.

I went along with everything, but inside, my body was saying, 'No!' Still, I was pushing past that and not listening to my intuition. I had put so much trust in this person; he was defining who I was. There were so many consequences for me in that. I allowed sexual and financial abuse. I allowed all my money to be lost.

There were niggling feelings that something was wrong. Every time I handed over $30,000, $50,000 and $100,000, I felt so sick in the guts. But then, he would say I just needed to open my mind because I was lacking in some way and couldn't manifest the things I needed. It was total gaslighting!

I was the last person I believed could be manipulated in this way because I thought I had power. I had the career. I had the money. I was sexually alluring. But in the end, I really had no power because I was so insecure and disconnected from my internal power. I wasn't listening to my intuition because of my shame. I lost it all trying to be accepted, trying to be what he defined as beautiful. That was not real power.

If you look at the heroine's journey, I hit the bottom of the well and lost everything. I stayed there trying to salvage everything and then came to a point where I could see that it was unsalvageable. But it was so much at the last minute.

I said to him, 'You've stolen my money.'

He looked me straight in the eyes and said, 'When I'm hungry, I eat.'

When Elissa shared this with me, I literally got a chill up my spine. Sexual power is such a complex phenomenon. I think it's only through stories that we're going to get a sense of it. Women are often too ashamed to discuss it, but we need to. When I look at Instagram and Facebook influencers, I see young women using that sexual power and labelling it as 'feminine power'. I can see they are using objectification of themselves and labelling it as powerful. That message is very simplistic and often misleading; they have no idea how consequential that is.

As I write this after hearing Elissa's story, I feel conflicted. As someone who enjoys my own sexuality and works in cultural dance where sexuality is a key ingredient to creative expression, I do not want to say to women, 'Don't be sexy' or 'Don't enjoy your body or your beauty'. I want to say embrace those things.

Is there a better way of wielding that power? Luckily, Elissa has greater wisdom to share.

Women have no idea how consequential sexual power is until it goes wrong. The work is really about a kind of awakening to the fact that there is insecurity underneath sexuality and this form of power. There is a shame wound underneath and fear of abandonment. So, rising to true feminine power is about tuning in to how you are in this moment. When you share those photos on Instagram or that video on TikTok, are you compensating for something? Ask yourself, 'How am I being in this moment? Am I in my dignity, or am I in my pride?'

If we drop into a deeper place and feel the heart space, there's wisdom. Dignity has a feeling to it; it's respectful, and it's got the heart included in it. It has awareness of our own well-being, of not hurting others, of having boundaries and respecting ourselves. Pride is more about what other people see and reflect back to you.

Beulah: Ending cycles of trauma

For Beulah, letting go of old power beliefs has been a lifelong pursuit of resilience and incredibly brave self-reflection. She realised that the story she was telling herself influenced her life, so she opted for a plot twist.

Thinking I wasn't smart enough to do the math kept me from studying psychology at first. But then, I got to a stage where I thought I'd give it a go and see what happens. That just started me on this path. It took me eight years to finish my PhD. I had some surgeries along the way, I had a daughter and a family to raise. I think I'm stubborn.

I reached a time in my life where I could see that I had ended that cycle of trauma, abuse, neglect and unhealthiness. With my daughter, I was starting something new. My daughter was free from that history; she was safe, and she was free. But I didn't see that that cycle stuck with me as well. I still hadn't gotten a sense of my power. I went through many years of thinking it was too late for me and that I would always be stuck there. I'm 45 now, and it's probably only in the last five years that I've recognised that the cycle can be broken with me, not just with her, and that I can own my power.

Part of that is being in my 40s. The older you get, the more you don't have the angst and the drama of your earlier years. And I'm loving my 40s because I care a lot less about the things that don't matter. I've started to get a sense that I do have control and power. I thought, What can I influence?

I realised that I've gone through my life story like a soap opera. The different things I've experienced would be quite a melodramatic life. So, I started saying to myself, 'If I'd gone through all of that, what can't I deal with?' That was a turning point for me. I realised I can change and that I can own this. I put in the hard work, and it's paying off.

The hard work is building that self-awareness and understanding yourself. It's the stuff everyone avoids because it's hard to look inwards to understand yourself, the way you work, what you're good at and what you're not so good at. It's the pain that's there, and recognising it and giving it space allows you to open up to others.

I'm so different now. If something happens, and I'm unhappy or stressed or anxious, I can tell that my mind is going in unhealthy ways. So, the first thing I do is reach out to a friend, which I never would have done before. Now I'm surrounded. I've collected this amazing group of women around me who are all works in progress. I'm also allowing myself to open up to the fact that they love me, value me, respect me and think I'm amazing. I'm still not comfortable with that, but I'm letting that in a little bit more.

The message given to me when I was little was that I wasn't worthy; I wasn't important. That I was an inconvenience, and I was in the way. So, it's taken a long, long time for me to shift from that.

LETTING GO OF OLD 'POWER' BELIEFS

Knowledge is power ... right?

Have you ever felt frustrated because now you have this knowledge but still don't feel powerful? What's going on? Our early experiences form our beliefs in adulthood about our gender roles, about who we should be as women and how we should behave. These beliefs are resistant to change. Letting go is hard sometimes. We sometimes can't imagine our lives without that role.

Often, our resistance to change is driven by a hidden commitment that contrasts with the change we are trying to make. In psychology, we call this a competing belief or commitment.[17] What are the beliefs you've committed to, leading to your resistance to change? For me, it was a belief that no matter what my father did, I was committed to being a 'good daughter'. This meant not speaking up, allowing myself to be subjugated to his wishes even in adulthood, and following a prescribed way of being a woman, even after I knew it didn't serve me or my values any longer.

It was only after many experiences with my father not meeting his obligation as a parent, or even just someone who respects me, that I finally realised it didn't make sense for me to be a good daughter anymore because he wasn't fulfilling his role as the 'good father'. Once that realisation came, I felt free. I could still feel love and forgiveness towards my father, but I no longer felt the obligation to the role expectations that had been part of my life for so long.

Change is hard; it takes energy, and it's painful sometimes. You must be clear about what you want to change, and remind yourself how you feel when you are your big, powerful, beautiful self.

What is the smallest first step you can take? Who can help you and keep you accountable? Eighty percent of life is about showing up; the rest happens after that. Where will you show up?

We sometimes don't show up because we're worried about what others will think; whether they'll continue to like us or even love us. Often, we can't say no even

---

[17] See Robert Kegan and Lisa Lahey's seminal work on Immunity to Change. https://hbr.org/2001/11/the-real-reason-people-wont-change.

when we know we should, because we consider others' needs before our own. This is a woman's unique strength: their communal, nurturing orientation. But it can also lead to self-limiting beliefs and barriers to change and growth.

Saying yes when you should say no or no when you should say yes can have devastating consequences. I made a life-altering decision when I was 27 years old – when I said yes, knowing it should have been a no. I married a man I knew I should not have married. I knew it in my gut, yet I couldn't act from a position of power at that time. I couldn't hurt him or disappoint our families. I felt that I was expected to be married and fulfil a significant milestone in a young woman's life. I felt the weight of all those expectations, of what was expected of me as a 'good daughter' and 'good wife', and then inevitably as a 'good mother'. But inside, I was screaming.

I remember being at the bridal designer's studio at my last wedding dress fitting. The wedding dress was my dream. It had cost way too much, but my father had given me the money so that I could purchase my perfect gown. It was made of royal Dutch satin with gorgeous gold trim. The dress was modern but had a flair of 18th century Madame de Pompadour. It had a straight pencil skirt from my waist to the floor below a bejewelled bodice, with metres of fabric creating a bustle in the back that flowed behind me into a golden-trimmed Dutch satin train. It was a stunning dress!

I was admiring myself in the mirror, alone in the dressing room after the designer had left to fetch my veil. I caught myself, and I heard the scream, 'NO!!!! Don't marry him!!!' But I had no tools at that time to speak up, to say no, to go against all those role expectations I was drowning under. Then I heard a song playing in my head – Once in a Lifetime, written and performed by the iconic '80s American rock band Talking Heads. It was a popular song at the time but not necessarily a favourite of mine. Yet, at that moment, the song lyrics spoke to me about finding myself in a place I thought was familiar, like a beautiful house, only to realise that it was not my beautiful house but one my gender role had prescribed. It was utterly disconnected from what I truly wanted for my life.

Despite what I knew, the marriage went ahead. Three years later, it was done. No children came into the relationship, which was a blessing. The divorce was not amicable, but also not the worst I've ever had!

After that, I went into a meltdown and came out of it with the help of several counsellors who helped me reflect on who I was and what I wanted for my life. I read many books that helped, some in psychology and others in spirituality. One of my favourites, which I still refer to today, is William Yuri's The Power of Positive No. It's a book I refer to all my clients, as many of them suffer from their own bias to saying yes.

Yuri provides a wonderful metaphor for learning to say no. He states that you need to be like a cherry tree. The roots of a cherry tree are long and deep, like our values, which drive our motivation and behaviours. The trunk is firm and solid. And the branches, when in bloom, are covered with blossoms, symbolising the many opportunities the cherry tree provides for beauty and growth.

When saying no, you can start by receiving the request in a way that shows you understand and value the person who requested the offer. Then, also express your values about the situation and how your values are aligned or misaligned with the request. For example, your boss may ask you to work late one weeknight too many, and you explain that you understand and care about your work responsibilities but have family responsibilities that, right now, are demanding your time.

The second step is to think about the cherry tree's solid and firm tree trunk when you express the no. But don't stop there; remember, there are cherry blossoms. Even though you can't say yes to the request, you can provide an opportunity for a way forward. For example, you could suggest some other time to complete the work or offer to work with your manager to find someone else who could complete the work. In this way, you are still showing that you care about the request and are willing to work with them to find a solution.

Chapter 6

All Girls Become Mothers, Don't They?

☆ ☆ ☆ ☆ ☆

Many women experience life-changing shifts in the face of becoming a mother, which in society, is an archetypal role for women. As this stage of life approaches, other conflicts become apparent, like juggling work and home responsibilities and shifting identities from woman to mother and back again. For women, it is an individual journey. And for those who do not go through the phase of motherhood, it is a journey of reclaiming their femininity in the absence of motherhood.

As an Italian woman, it took me a long time to come to terms with my status as a woman without biological children. I tolerated many pitying looks from relatives as they surmised there must be something wrong with me. Even after almost a decade of postgraduate study and being the first person in my extended family to achieve a PhD, the women in my family – including my mother – were relieved that now the study was done, I could get down to the real purpose of my life, which was to have children. I remember many conversations where I was back-pedalling, hating myself for saying things like, 'No, I really do like children', 'Yes, I did try, but it didn't happen for me', and 'Maybe one day' – all feeble attempts to defend my feminine identity against a standard I wasn't signed up to.

There is no positive term in English for me as a childfree woman. Many other cultures use the term *Aunty*, ascribed to a female elder who is not your biological mother but commands the same respect. In Italian, it's *Zia*.

I am Aunty to my sister's three children whom I love to the moon and back, and I grew up with many Zias. Still, it took me a long time to come to terms with who I was as a woman without going through motherhood.

I'm not here to say something is wrong with motherhood, only that motherhood being a prerequisite to femininity is a misattribution. I believe fulfilling the role of mother can be a superpower for some and a time when women discover their internal power. Yet, as you will read in the following stories, this was not always the case for others. And for some, the potential for motherhood is already conceived as a competing commitment to the career goals young women are striving for.

Rachel: Motherhood is a superpower

For Rachel, the journey into motherhood was one of empowerment and discovering true inner strength.

> *The feeling of power when you have a baby is like nothing on earth. You feel invincible, almost like Superwoman, because you think, 'I just created a human, and I gave birth to that human.' Even just raising children takes huge strength. It's such a challenging role, and no one really knows what they're doing. You figure it out as you go, and there is one thing that is a gift women have for children – nurturing with unconditional love.*

> *So many things about women are strength-based and powerful. Every experience adds to your power if you know how to use it. Career-wise, it's taken me a while as a woman to feel like I'm taken seriously in my work. That's probably more of an internal belief around confidence, which stems from growing up female. The*

conditioning women have to overcome to recognise that our feminine qualities are strengths and not weaknesses is enormous.

I still remember being told in Year 9 that the only career path I could follow was a teacher or a nurse. I remember thinking, 'I don't want to be either of those things. Am I the only one who's ambitious around here?' A lot of my friends were ambitious, but we weren't encouraged to be. So, I think the power that comes from ambition is that feeling of being driven, wanting to be better and wanting to achieve.

Lucia: Assuming the burden of caring

Many of the younger women I spoke with while writing this book held a tacit belief that they would bear the burden of primary caregiving when they chose to have a family and children. It is an assumption that seemed unquestioned for the most part.

Lucia is a force to be reckoned with and has been since starting her first business as a teenager. She thrives in her business and loves the role of Founder. She reflects on the support she will need to fulfil her dream of a happy family and business.

When she looks ahead, she believes it is her responsibility to create a work lifestyle where she can either leave work altogether to raise children or work part-time.

I definitely want to be a mother. I want to have a happy life. I want to be a speaker, travel the world, write a book and have more fun.

My work is so much fun, but I also need to be okay without my work. Without that, who am I? I do put my work first, almost as a safety net, because I know that so well. That's why, I guess, I worked so hard for so long at the start. I wanted to get my business to a level where I could be part-time when I have a family. That's what I'm still working on. I want more time for kids because I know you have to be there for them. You have to have that time. But I also think having a nanny is a good option.

> *There's so much going on all the time that it's hard because it takes a village to raise a child. So, creating that village of support with family, with business, with colleagues and with nannies is important. Just changing the way society sees it all is my vision.*
>
> *What was beautiful during Covid is that we saw so many women with their kids at work. I love how people have conversations about how women have so many roles. Being a mum is a full-time job and a half, so I just love how people say, 'Why don't we make it easier for women? How will we make it easier for them?'*
>
> *I love the conversations coming through now, and it will take a few more generations until there's a solution, but I love where it's heading.*

Olivia: Planning her career around work and family

Despite being in her early career, Olivia is already planning for a significant career in leadership. At the same time, she is also reflecting on how she will manage the inevitable career break due to having children.

Despite not even having a partner yet, she is viewing the work–life–family juggle solely from her perspective as a woman and within the traditional feminine role expectations that are so entrenched as to be invisible.

> *I have started to think about what's next. I'm still thinking it through, to be honest. I'm reflecting on where I get the most value and meaning from the work and thinking back on things I like doing, like coaching and supporting people's development and even team facilitation. I love all of that and getting that rewarding feeling.*
>
> *When it comes to having kids, I have thought about and wondered if I would stop working for several years and focus on them. I'm also hoping to get to a more senior level before that pause in my career comes, so then it's easy to pick up again.*

Justine: I don't have it all together

For Justine, who is a mother of young children and a highly sought-after HR Consultant, author and speaker, juggling home and work is a question of how to live by your values in an imperfect world.

Women will start off, and they are just so conscientious – not to say men aren't. But as a woman, you love your career, and you'll give it everything. Then you have a family, and if you find that you can't give as much as you could before, you are pulled into all these different directions. You don't want to lose your heart. You've got this huge heart wanting to give as much as you can, but it's not physically possible. So, you ask, 'Where do I fail less?' which is the worst feeling in the world. All that does is make you feel worse because you're high on accountability and not blaming anyone else but yourself.

You wonder, 'What am I doing wrong here?' You're at home, and you're fantastic. You're capable of being this incredible person, but how do you live into your values? You're also capable of this great professional success that you want at the same time. So, you ask yourself, 'What is my value?' and it becomes quite a complex, ongoing conversation.

How do you become fully self-expressed at this moment? How do you give yourself the confidence to speak up fully when you're not necessarily getting the signals that you should speak about it because it's probably a lot more comfortable for everyone else that you stay quiet and keep pedalling?

That's always why when another woman asks me how I do it all, I try to disappoint her a little bit. It's sort of a duty to say, 'Well, I'm not all together.' That's really important. Because if you show you're together, that's one of the falsehoods you share. If you pretend you're perfect, it's a false picture you're perpetuating.

Dina: I'm so sorry; we tried to call your wife ...

Dina, an ambitious and accomplished mid-career HR professional, has always had 'ridiculously high standards' for herself.

When it comes to how I parent and my friendships and romantic relationships, I place very high expectations on myself and others, probably because of the multiple roles I try to play. I have two kids; my daughter is eight, and my son is five. I was 29 when I had my first. That's a young age to be a mother. Nothing can ever really prepare you for becoming a parent. Still, I could have done with a few more years of life experience.

If I were going back, we wouldn't necessarily do it again. There's this expectation to reproduce, but there isn't enough education about what it means to be a parent and how to make an educated and informed decision on whether that's a path for you. I'm certainly not one of those people who say having children changed my life. I mean, it certainly changed my lifestyle, that's for sure.

When I think back, there was no pressure from my family to have kids, but there's this unspoken pressure we have as a society and a stereotype that it's your responsibility as a woman. Otherwise, what are you equal to? There's no other value for women unless you're going to reproduce, right? It just sounds so awful. And I say it that way because it bothers me so much, and it's only now that I'm a grown-up, in my late 30s, that I am properly questioning it. Like, why? Where did this pressure come from? Where did I feel this need to fulfil that responsibility to be a parent?

There's such a responsibility in having kids. They take up so much of your time and resources, and so the time you have for yourself is very limited and therefore valuable. Then, you start to think you have so little time to do these things that drive and motivate you; you better make sure they're things you're passionate about. With all the stresses and pressures that come with parenting, how hard would it be to go into a job you hate or a job that doesn't drive you or you don't really believe in. That would be tough.

After having my kids, I took some time off work, but I found that really hard to do. I found the entire experience of having kids, and the shock that it was, hard to adjust to.

You have this romantic idea about what it means to have children when you get married; you're in love and high on those hormones. You have a certain illusion that it's a biological imperative in so many ways. You have this desire to procreate without having a full comprehension of what it means.

I found the pregnancies hard, and I wasn't one of those people that enjoyed being pregnant at all. I hated every minute of it. I didn't feel in control, had no idea what was happening, and found staying home difficult. I stayed at home for about nine months each time, and it was extremely isolating and lonely.

The expression 'It takes a village to raise a child' is right, but we don't have the village anymore. The village is gone. We're all alone. Your partner gets up in the morning, goes off to work, and returns at 6 pm or 7 pm, while you've been alone all day with a very demanding baby.

You feel so disconnected from the real world because everything comes to such an abrupt stop. You've had a career where you've interacted with people; you've had that intellectual stimulation every day. Suddenly, you're just this baby machine at home: you're feeding, changing, trying to put them to sleep and figuring out what's happening, all the while feeling insecure about it and questioning yourself.

The transition back to work was difficult as well. Even though nine months probably doesn't sound like a very long time, you feel quite wobbly in the real world of work. It's like learning to walk all over again. There's also a bit of that mother-guilt kicking in: I went back to work, which means I'll be spending less time with my baby, and my baby is still small. It's selfish to leave my young baby, so I feel guilty prioritising myself when I go back to work.

It's hard going back to work, thinking people will look at you differently. Your priorities change. For a little while, you have no choice because small kids get sick a lot. The expectation is that you're the responsible one rather than your partner or husband. It's always the mothers that get called.

My husband and I always laugh about this, even to this day. When my daughter is unwell in school, the school always calls me first. Then, when they call my partner, they say, 'Sorry, Mr W; we tried to call your wife, but she didn't pick up.'

So, that's a lot to deal with. You're dealing with that mother's guilt whilst also dealing with that expectation. How do I do both roles? How do I do work?

As a woman, you know you're the primary caregiver, whatever that means. I hate that expression. It's not like you get a bigger slice of your child, and they take more of your DNA. You know, they take 23 chromosomes from either parent; I really don't understand where the whole primary and secondary caregiver nonsense comes from, but that's the society we live in.

We've not designed jobs to cater to flexible working, which is the real disconnect. The team I work in is wonderful. My manager does not micromanage in any way; I don't even need to let her know if I've got a sick child and have to stay at home, or if I've got to finish up early or start late. I manage my own diary. And I'm the same way with my team. I don't expect them to let me know they've got a sick kid and have to log off. I don't care. It's about the work you're delivering, not how.

But, in so many ways, I still see that push. And again, I just want to reiterate, they are so brilliant in my organisation. They showed this in the return-to-office policy – whatever works for you and your team. But you still get the vibe that big corporates haven't gotten their head around the fact that work has changed. The office is dead. When will they finally acknowledge that many employees don't want to be in the office?

Still, they are sending the signals and symbols that they appreciate it if you come into the office. I'm all for it. Don't get me wrong; I love going into the office, interacting with people and spending that face-to-face time, but I can see the value of both working from home and the office. I can see how we can collaborate well when we come together, but I can also see how it works for me to have the flexibility to work from home, duck in and out, and get other things done along the way. So, yeah, we've still got a long way to go in corporate Australia.

Elissa: This is boring, he said

Elissa thought she had a good plan. She would continue fast-tracking her career while her husband took on the caring role when their child arrived. The plan went ahead for a while … until he got bored.

My body clock just started ticking. Actually, it wasn't even the body clock; the conditioning kicked in. You're already in your early 20s, and it's time to get married, have babies, and buy a home. So, I got married. But the deal I made with my husband then was that I'm no stay-at-home mum. I know that I needed a career. I wanted to make money. I wanted to spend money. I wanted to have a good life. And I still wanted to have children. My partner said he wanted to be a stay-at-home husband, so it was all good.

I was expecting to go back to my career after having the baby, but he changed his mind and said, 'This is boring. I'm not doing it.' So, I had to drop my career – well, I felt like I had to. 'If he's not doing it, I must do it because I'm the mother. In fact, I should have been doing it in the first place!'

I stepped into that role, but I always felt misplaced. I felt discontented. I felt like my brain was going to mush. It wasn't good. And then, I left him. I left him when I was in my mid-30s. I took the kids, and I walked away from my own life. I decided to create a new life, which was more based on my energy, because I hadn't matured in the world.

Being a migrant, I wasn't allowed to go out, stay with friends overnight, or move out of home. My mother said, 'Sure, you can move out if you want to, but you take nothing with you, and you never come back.'

The consequence for me was that when I got married, I hadn't really matured into the world as an individual. I still had to individuate. As a woman in my mid-30s with two children and all that responsibility, I was trying to figure out what it is to be a single mature woman in the world.

These stories confirm what many of us have experienced. We have defined work and personal life by attempting to obtain a balance between the time we spend at work and everything else. This view sees these parts of our lives as separate and independent and assumes that we can flip from one to the other. However, women define career, power and leadership through how they feel about their career and their lives as a whole.

In attempting to strike a balance between their relationships with others and their personal achievements at work, women seek personal satisfaction or meaning in both realms. The desire to fulfil occupational and interpersonal roles is particularly true of high-achieving women.[18] Therefore, women with high expectations of home and work often seek occupations that accommodate both.

The balance metaphor is unhelpful, however. Living our best lives is not about getting a balance between work and home as if they can be compartmentalised. It's about bringing our whole self to everything we do, where there's no distinction between work, home and life. It's all you! It's all you at work, and you at home. It's you raising children. It's you involved in your community. It's you involved in leading others and in following others.

It's just life; there's no balance to be had. It's about prioritising every day in every week. We wake up valuing all those aspects of ourselves, not just one aspect over the other. In other words, we don't value work over home tasks; they have equal value in our life.

The problem with the balance metaphor is that it sees different aspects of our lives as separate. The balance view is a masculine or agentic way of perceiving ourselves because it forces independence across these aspects of our lives, which are, in fact, interdependent and connected. What we need is a connected view of ourselves and our lives, not a dichotomous view of ourselves.

We have defined not only work but everything else we do in life according to a masculine modality. The consequences of this can be seen in the way we value activity in one domain over the other. We still don't value domestic labour. It is not in the interest of men or masculinity to value domestic labour because, globally, they are not doing that work.

---

[18] JM Adams, When working women become pregnant. New England Business, vol 6, 1984, pp 18-21

ALL GIRLS BECOME MOTHERS, DON'T THEY?

As a senior leader, I rejected this dichotomy. I was in the process of recruiting a Senior Communications Officer into my team and was in the final stages of deciding between two great candidates. During this process, one of the candidates, Kate, asked to see me to disclose what she thought may disadvantage her from getting the role. She said, 'I need to let you know that I'm four months pregnant. I understand if that's a deal-breaker for getting this role.'

Kate told me later that my response was a complete surprise to her. I replied, 'Wow, that's amazing! Congratulations!' and proceeded to tell her that I was excited about the skills she would learn through the journey of having her first child and how those strengths would contribute to this role rather than be a disadvantage. I reassured her that we could backfill the role during whatever maternity leave arrangements she might choose to have if she was the successful candidate and confirmed that she was still very much in line to securing this position.

I hired Kate as the best candidate for the role, and she joined our team, taking nine months of maternity leave after having the baby. We used the opportunity to give another staff member in the wider team an opportunity for a lateral movement into this role, which also increased the team's capability in specialised communications. It was a win-win.

I wish we lived in a world where Kate needn't feel scared to tell a prospective employer that she is pregnant. I wish for a world where leaders perceive the incredible learning journey of having a child and parenthood as advantageous to our work lives rather than a burden.

Think about the skills and growth new parents experience as they face these new challenges. Why don't we acknowledge this in work and leadership? Why don't we see the new role that women and men adopt in their personal lives as significant benefits to the roles they fulfil in their work lives? Instead of seeing these dual roles as conflicting with each other and needing 'balancing', why don't we see these dual roles as interdependent and enhancing both our work and personal lives?

Sue, on men as primary carers

Even though Sue was the primary breadwinner for her young family, the primary caring role for her children was relegated to her rather than her partner. She envisions a future where men are expected to take on more responsibility for family caring.

What I wish for younger women now is a workplace where they don't feel so torn. I had so much guilt, particularly in the relationship. You know that mother's guilt? I was the major breadwinner. I ended up having to return to work or work more hours than I wanted to because it was a financially sensible decision. I was earning double – triple, at one point – than my husband.

Men are allowed the freedom to shirk the responsibility of domestic labour. I've known for a long time that there will not be gender equality until men have the same ability and desire to take on parental and other home responsibilities without penalty to your career. It's not only childcare but also elder care. My parents are no longer alive, but I see all my friends looking after their elders and, as they're parents become less able to look after themselves, having to make decisions about their long-term care is really challenging.

Our organisational designs assume that we all work full-time, and it's an anomaly to work part-time or in different ways, right? When we design roles, we tend to design them with a full-time person in mind when in reality you have two people job-sharing or two part-time people. It's about the volume. So, we assume that if someone is not full-time, they can be discriminated against or passed over in promotion rounds, or things are organised when they're not there. And processes are designed in the organisation with an assumption that everyone is there Monday to Friday, 9 am to 5 pm.

Chapter 7

Get Your Boss Pants On; We Need You

☆ ☆ ☆ ☆ ☆

We know that women excel as managers and CEOs. But when we look at the statistics, the proportion of world leaders and women on boards is low, with women holding heads of state positions in only 22 countries. Representation of women in government is only 21% globally and 36% in local government. Globally, in 2019, women only held 28% of managerial positions. It was a little better in Australia and New Zealand at 38%.

Since 2000, the rate of women in managerial positions has increased in most regions, but the rate of improvement is slight. Women CEOs represent only 18% of the total population, with more women employed in junior management rather than senior management roles.[19] This is indicative of the glass ceiling many women face in management roles.

---

[19] Global Gender Gap Report 2020, World Economic Forum, Switzerland, 2019, https://www.weforum.org/reports/gender-gap-2020-report-100-years-pay-equality.

I refer to our Lasso of Truth in this book because women have the potential to create a new generation of more communal cooperative leaders. The current global problems we face will only be solved with greater collaboration, so we need the kind of leadership that enables that. Emerging leaders tend to learn from other leaders around them, who are already behaving in a way that successfully got them promoted.

When they look up the leadership ladder, they see competitive and individualistic characteristics in these leaders. These behaviours are the antithesis of cooperation and collaboration. Many organisations are addressing this issue in their leadership cultures right now. Still, we've got a long way to go to achieve collaborative leadership as a norm in major Western corporations.

Successful experiences in leadership build greater capability and confidence in leadership. Some women are not rewarded for their competency and are overlooked due to perceived attributes about their leadership ability. Yet, the research data clearly shows that women can lead and, when given the opportunity, lead well.

Earlier in this book, I spoke about my upbringing and how I had very few female role models that were career-oriented. However, when I look back on my mother's efforts to successfully run a business after facing many challenges herself, I must admit that she showed me the pathway to my own future entrepreneurship.

Lina: Selling Mary Kay

Lina, my mother, is less traditional than other Italian mothers of her generation. She is more open, broad-minded and street smart – some of that she was born with, and some came from her unique life circumstances. She migrated to Australia on her own when she was only 18 years old and was divorced with three children years later, at a time when the Italian community in Australia shunned divorced women.

After leaving her marriage, Lina began working independently for companies that required in-home hosted parties, such as Mary Kay Cosmetics, Homewares and even Tupperware. In-home sales were a big deal pre-digital, and this was many years before the internet. Despite having very rudimentary written English skills at that time, she was very successful and even made top State Salesperson for Mary Kay one month, which got her a pink car as a bonus! I remember her being so proud of that! She was able to support all of us and eventually bought our family home – and she did it all on her own.

Lina was such a force! I remember she stopped the car once when we were out for groceries because she saw two young women walking along the footpath. She approached them with a big, warm smile and asked, 'Have you heard of Mary Kay? I think you'd really like them,' and proceeded to book a host party! I, of course, was mortified sitting in the car watching this, but this was just how she was. She never let an opportunity for a sale slip by.

I learned boldness, resilience and independence from my mother. Yet, at the time, I wouldn't have called her entrepreneurial. It was only when looking back at all the obstacles she overcame, including her struggles with depression then, that I realised how determined she must have been to keep going. She transferred that entrepreneurial spirit to us kids. Even today, it's a big influence on our lives.

Ilona: Being 100% myself in a leadership role

Ilona discovered true feminine power in an HR Director role where she could be 100% herself. I'm sure that men never even think about being 100%, or any other portion, of themselves in leadership because stereotypes globally inform us that leader or manager equates with being male.

> *I took on the best role I've ever had, which was the Chief People Officer role for an organisation that I knew very little about at the time. It was a technology company that the Oracle founders have since bought. It was the first role that I have ever felt truly myself in and where I could be 100% myself. I didn't need to put on any different personas. I'd still adjust my style for board meetings, but that's where I felt I had my power. That is where I finally came into my own because I felt truly comfortable with who I was.*

Although I was very confident the rest of the time, it didn't mean I was comfortable all the time. At that organisation, they were like sponges; they wanted to learn, grow, take what I knew, and help the company and themselves. In that context, I just thrived. It made me reflect and think, How on earth did I last all that time in corporate life?

Yes, this is a tech company; it's fast-paced and has a higher level of risk-taking. There were not so many rules; they didn't like rules at all. In fact, that was part of my interview with them. They said, 'I hope you're not going to come in and put all these HR rules in place.' I reassured them that it's not how I work. I'm quite rebellious.

Rebecca: Leadership allows me to help more people

Rebecca discovered that leadership was a collective rather than individualistic concept. Her leadership purpose was to help and develop others.

I never sought recognition from Salesforce for helping other people in the community. I just wanted to ensure that other people didn't feel as lost as I did when I first started using Salesforce. Using this technology platform changed my life, so I wanted to give them an opportunity to experience what I had in the community, help them be trusted and respected in their organisation, and help them find mentors or be a mentor to them. That's always been my goal – to help people feel included, seen and valued.

As I've gotten more experience in leadership positions, it's allowed me to help more people. So, my drive is helping others to have a better day and to help people when they come to work in the morning. If I look back at all my roles, all of them have been about helping others get better at whatever they're doing.

Tina: Collective leadership

Tina believes her impact is better made outside of the C-suite. Her idea of leadership is collective, like Rebecca's, and she articulates her vision for an organisation that is flatter, devoid of hierarchy and modelled on self-managed teams.

I've been told for many years that there's no reason why you can't be General Manager or be in the C-suite. But I didn't get there, not because I didn't have the competency, but more so because I didn't have that drive. So, I report to the C-suite. I do aspire to be a leader who inspires whatever role I'm in by how I can inspire others to get shit done.

Leadership is quite limiting at this point in my career. I don't think there would be barriers if that's where I wanted to head, but I don't think I want to climb the tree. I want to inspire others and not have barriers around that, and I do see that hierarchy is designed with constraints.

Slowly, though, more and more organisations are starting to challenge that. They are asking what value hierarchical structures actually add. And so, I aspire that more organisations, including my own, explore these ideas. I'd love to one day work in an organisation where you're rewarded for your contribution, not by your level in the hierarchy.

I'd be putting myself in a box in an executive leadership role. Where I currently fit in the organisation, I can navigate up and out and inspire down. If I got any higher, I'd lose touch with the true power.

True power is with the people you need to empower, the people at the coalface. You need to speak to the people attaching the product to the services and touching the customers every day. They've got the answer.

I love being in a place where I can engage with those people, find answers by working with them and see them be inspired. In one of the more recent projects we worked on, I got an email from one of the guys on the shop floor. He said, 'I just want to thank you for not only listening to our feedback about the tool we were building together but actually taking it on board and turning it around.'

This email just blew me away. In the past, people had come and asked them for their input and feedback but never came back or applied it.

I had a chance to contact a friend who's a CEO of a not-for-profit organisation where she's applying the whole concept of self-managed teams – a concept also mentioned in the book I've been listening to, called Humanocracy.

I've been amazed as I've been listening to how many different types of organisations apply it. I thought it might only apply in the health or services industry, but quite a few heavy industry businesses, like a steel business in the United States, apply the concept too. It's been twisting my mind how you would apply this in real life within an organisation. It would take a lot of courage from all layers and levels.

One of the concepts I love is where your peers do your performance review, giving accountability to the people at the frontline to make decisions about reward and recognition for the team.

Let's say we were going to put a new piece of equipment in a part of the manufacturing shop. Typically, this needs a business case approved by all the appropriate levels. In the world of self-managed teams, the people using the equipment do the research and can make these decisions. The examples I have been pondering suggest that if they are remunerated by outcomes, their collaborative decisions are more likely to drive the types of yields and successes the business is striving for. It's a very different way of thinking. So, it flips everything on its head.

The other thing that I think is exciting and critical to business improvement is having coaches amongst the masses – people who coach others on how to have those courageous conversations. For instance, they help if you're looking to make a change but have some conflict with other team members, and you need to navigate those and try and work your way through that.

I love this concept of building the capability to have those conversations at the layers that matter. It's not rocket science, but for so many businesses today, the hierarchy does constrain us. There's so much power within every person, but we don't tap into that enough.

We're an organisation of many individuals, and we all have so much to bring to the table. We have so much untapped knowledge and experience because people don't want to speak up, or because they feel like they'll get shut down or it's not their place to say. You hear people say, 'That's above my paygrade', which is the worst thing ever! It says so much about your organisation's culture when people say that. That's just so sad, isn't it?

The mindset 'That's beyond my paygrade' is a very individual way of perceiving the world, or at least an employee's role within their organisation. It's a view devoid of an awareness of the interconnectedness between all parts of the organisation and an individual's contribution to a connected end-to-end value chain.

This mindset is a symptom of a work system that has been fashioned in a very masculine and agentic way. Masculinity, when expressed in a system, is that drive for independence and individualism. In contrast, positive femininity drives interdependence and communion, viewing all things as part of the same ecosystem.

Chapter 8

Unleashing Your Power
☆ ☆ ☆ ☆ ☆

Many women I interviewed for this book described a moment in their life when they had either raised awareness of or increased desire to finally release the power they had suppressed. These stories of transformation are uniquely Individual and powerful parables of the changes women go through once they step into their true feminine power.

Rachel: What doesn't kill you makes you stronger

I've always known that contrast makes you stronger. Unfortunately, this becomes apparent only after the trauma, sadness or strife we all go through. It's only in hindsight that the wisdom and insight become apparent for some – like Rachel after her divorce. This catalyst started a change in her, as she discovered a feminine vulnerability that was key to her strength and power.

> *It took the total upheaval of my life to truly understand myself and what I am capable of. Recently, I've been through a marriage separation, and it absolutely tested my strength like you wouldn't believe. I see that as power moving in a lot*

of ways. In some ways, I did it for myself, even though I had to consider everyone in the process. I knew I wasn't happy where I was and needed to do something about it. Taking that step was the biggest and hardest decision I had ever made. Even though it was absolutely devastating, it gave me power and strength.

I needed to move out of my comfort zone. I got married quite young and had relied on someone else since. That was the thing missing for me – I wasn't relying on myself. That was possibly one of the reasons, the catalyst for many other things, but it certainly was difficult for me the last two years.

I was questioning myself all the time. I knew deep down that I wasn't happy, but I couldn't put my finger on why – I still don't totally know why. But I've got some theories: The catalyst for my decision was to find inner strength.

I had done a lot of work on myself over the last few years with a coach and had a lot more awareness of myself and my needs. I came to the realisation that I had put all my needs aside for so many years; it was time that I focussed on myself and understood what I wanted. I'm allowed to have a happy life. I did work with a counsellor, as well, who helped me see that I am allowed to be happy. I was always bad at asking for help and soon realised, after deep reflections on myself, that I was a people pleaser. I think that's probably one of the downfalls of being a strong but also caring and kind person. Even though you have that strength and power, sometimes you forget to ask for help and to say no, because you think it's weak or you're being vulnerable.

My coach helped me understand that being vulnerable is okay – though, I still fight it. It's about understanding your feminine side and your masculine side. Because I've had to deal with so many different things in my life, I probably have leaned towards the masculine side and tried to stay strong. But now I feel like I need to discover my feminine side, and that's a new, powerful thing for me.

The divorce was a turning point in my life, a major turn, and I realised I needed to change personally and professionally. I started focussing on mastering seven areas of my life: family and friends, professional, spirituality, lifestyle, health and fitness, financial and relationships. I journal every day to stay focussed on each one.

I had also been to a course a few years before, where I met my coach. I started talking to this guy sitting next to me; he was Scottish. I have Scottish heritage, and I felt like he was somehow sent to help me through a very dark period of my life. So, I started chatting with him, and I experienced a very profound shift in my consciousness and awareness. He explained to me that I was ready to be awakened and that I have a gift. He then became my coach and helped me unpack a whole heap of stuff that I'd been holding onto from my youth.

The whole experience with him inspired me to become a coach so I could help others transform their lives and move on from trauma and sadness. My life coach helped me understand that it's okay to be vulnerable, even though I still fight it and feel the need to be in control. It's about understanding your old story and feeling empowered to write your new story – to change the narrative, align with your feminine side and your masculine side and find the equilibrium of both.

Because I've had to deal with so many different things in my life, I probably have leaned towards the masculine side and tried to stay strong. But now I feel like I need to discover my feminine side, and that's a new thing for me. I think that's a powerful thing in itself, having this knowledge to transform to find balance and peace.

Rebecca: A super heavyweight woman

Like Rachel, Rebecca came to significant changes in her life after her divorce. She worked on gaining power in a very tangible way, which led to winning gold medals in Powerlifting Championships for Australia.

I got divorced about 10 years ago or so. At that time, I was unhappy with my life and everything going on with it. So, I started powerlifting. Now I'm a competitive powerlifter and strongwoman. I've represented Australia twice and won gold medals in Powerlifting Championships for Australia in Slovakia and Hungary.

Lifting in the last 10 years is a journey that's shown me I'm more capable than I think I am. It has given me purpose and support along with the community that goes along with lifting.

I'm a super heavyweight woman. When I first started lifting, there weren't a lot of super heavyweight women in strength sports in Australia because women do care about how they look. When you put on a soft suit and stand on the lifting platform, you're bare. It's a very tight, short onesie suit, and it doesn't hide any of your rolls or bumps or lumps – it's all out there for show.

Many super heavyweight women who have gone into the sport have looked to me and said, 'Thank you. I wasn't able to do that on the platform until I saw someone else doing that.'

I'm now finding generations of lifters I inspired into the sport in the last 10 years. Generations of strongwomen and women doing powerlifting are doing it because I led the way 10 years ago. That's exciting!

Last year I took an unofficial Australian record at bench press. At the start of last year, I took the Queensland record for bench press for master's women. Back in 2012 to 2017, I would probably train four nights a week, up to two to three hours each night. I was trying to work back into being non-competitive for a little while, but I found it challenging because I have such a drive for competitiveness. I have a drive to challenge myself and be better.

The same themes come through into my leadership role. I'm challenging myself, being better than I was yesterday, and not being shy to be myself along the way – that's the leadership shadow you need to own and step into. That leadership shadow and doing what you do is what other people see. If they respect that, they follow you, which is really a great feeling!

Pauline, on authentic leadership

Pauline shows her authentic self in expressing care to her staff. She tells several stories wherein she has expressed intense emotion at work, during a high and a low in the organisation, and how she would never have been able to express that authenticity earlier in her career.

We were building a business from scratch. My team did a demo of some of the systems customers will use.

As the demo progressed, we started to get all these messages from the staff, like 'This is amazing' and 'Oh my god, you guys have done so much in such a short period'. I got overwhelmed and emotional. I'm aware that people see me as the new CEO, and expectations come with that.

Anyway, in the end, the facilitator of the meeting asked me if there was anything I wanted to say. I started gushing and talking about the staff's comments, the journey we've taken, and how I feel about my team and their work.

I was surprised I was bawling my eyes out, but I didn't care. I realised people didn't know me and may also be judging me, but it was fine. I was fine being me and expressing my feeling and emotions.

It happened again the other day when we had just done an Employee Engagement Survey, and some pretty negative results came through, enterprise-wide. I really took that to heart.

And so, I got emotional during that presentation as well, talking about some of the things we need to work out and need to do. I wouldn't have been okay with showing so much emotionality earlier in my career, though. It wasn't seen as a good thing. In fact, I was often criticised, and it impacted my performance reviews at the time.

I'm now seeing people around me change their expectations of leaders because of what I'm role modelling. I think people are responding better to it. Even other leaders are changing. For example, another executive said to me, 'You're very different from me, Pauline. I can learn a lot from you. You feel more. You share your emotions, you hug – I don't do that. I like that, though. I need to do more of it.'

Nicole finds leadership in the desert

For Nicole, it took a relationship with a First Nations mob to begin unravelling and unleashing her inner power, which had been tied up in cultural expectations of herself as a Chinese woman. Spending time in the Australian desert with an Aboriginal family seeking their own justice helped her unravel the cultural boundaries that had kept her thinking small and subservient for so many years.

I've spent many years in the desert, and it was a turning point in my development as a person. I had never met an Aboriginal person up to the point when I went out to start shooting the film. I met them because I was working at the museum and had to meet Aboriginal people to consult on some exhibits. What I got was a pitch on an idea for the film. They realised, especially Dolly, how film can help tell their story – for it to be recorded and passed on to future generations.

They said I could come and film and that they were going 'back to country' after 50 years. You know, everyone talks about our connection to country, but what does that mean? I worked with them for 10 years, yet I just scratched the surface. I understood perhaps half of what they were telling me, but it took me that long to get a grip on my slight understanding of what their story meant so I could then interpret it.

I was born in Australia but left when I was 3 months old. My family moved to Hong Kong, and my sisters were born there, and then we went to Singapore, where I grew up. My childhood was in Southeast Asia before I returned to Australia when I was 13 years old.

When our family was living in Hong Kong, we were very close. We'd spend a lot of time there even after we left. We'd go back there for the holidays. We had our extended family in Hong Kong, and we had our life in Australia. Those two things were very confusing, and I was culturally confused. It was hard to understand who I was. I only now understand the impact of thinking that I'm Chinese all my life. I now realise I'm not Chinese; I'm Chinese Australian. It's a huge difference.

It's been difficult realising this now that I'm looking back on all the cultural boundaries and the way the culture has imposed its structure and its fundamental thinking on me as a woman. It still is in my DNA.

Most of my life, when I embarrassingly look back on it now, I have at times played that role. I lived in New York for 13 years, and you know, in America, they have a strange attitude towards racism and Chinese and Blacks and all that sort of thing. To rebel against that cultural template, I married a Black man.

Elissa shuts down her sexual energy

Current stereotypes associated with women collapse career, family and sexuality into the same bowl of expectation and fulfilment for women. Not only do we expect to have a full career, but we also expect ourselves to be the perfect mother, wife, daughter and seductress, along with the many other roles attributed to us in society.

Elissa learned this through her own heroine's journey. She felt powerful in the role of mother, in her career and in her sexuality, with the latter being a critical aspect of her power. Striving for perfection in all three roles, she erred in hubris, which made her blind to the true power of her inner knowing or voice.

I was feeling empty. With wealthy men chasing me around, I was doing 'sexy' and feeling empty. I went overseas on a long trip with a girlfriend. It was more of a spiritual journey, like the Camino Frances, where Christian pilgrims walk around 800 km on a path treaded by revered saints thousands of years ago and pay homage to religious relics along the way. We went to the south of France for a spiritual experience and timeout. When I came back, I broke it off with my boyfriend and didn't date anybody. I burned all my black, lacy underwear and wore white cotton as my secret symbol, just for myself, that I wasn't going to use my sexuality in that way anymore.

I shut down my sexuality, so much so that I got sick. I developed thyroidism – it was all burnout. Sexual energy has a purpose, right? I got physically sick because I was clamping down on that sexual energy. I hadn't quite worked out how to constructively use it.

I thought I had worked it out when I delved into sacred sexuality. I practised it for four years. Three women worked for me, and we taught sacred sexuality. I had 1,200 clients – all men. They were all powerful men – barristers, lawyers, scientists, doctors and accountants. I connected them to their own bodies.

Here I was with my girls, trying to teach these men how to honour a woman and respect the whole energy, which was really the conversation I wanted to have with my father. I absorbed it without knowing that there was disrespect with how he treated my mother when I was growing up. Some part of me knew that it was his disrespect I was addressing. The women that worked for me moved from the profane to the sacred in that work. This shift was symbolic. In the end, that business had to close.

I realised it was all about those sexual energies being misplaced.

So, I had 12 months of celibacy, wearing white underwear and working on my health. During that time, I had realisations about how I unconsciously misused my sexuality because of my insecurities, even though I was never promiscuous. I just wasn't understanding the energy itself.

I knew that energy had to be tamed. I decided to completely change my life. At the time, I knew everything had to change. I sold all the bits and pieces and wanted to start fresh. But while I was doing all that, my spiritual teacher at the time said, 'Look, it's time that you go out and put love and laughter and joy back into your life.'

I had an event to go to, a girlfriend's birthday. There were about 50 people in the room, and I was standing up against the wall, feeling a bit numb, and not really interacting with anyone. Then something from inside of me said, 'Okay then, if you really want change, what would you do differently in this moment?'

I looked around the room and saw a man wearing bright-coloured clothing and jovially chatting with people on the other side of the room. I went through it in my head, thinking that having a conversation with that man would probably be gross because he was almost childlike. When I say childlike, I mean he exuded pure innocence rather than alpha-male energy.

So, I had a conversation with this man, and his energy picked me up. Fast forward to now, and we got married. That's when I also left my job and went back to school full-time.

I loved this conversation with Elissa because I have also experienced the many sides of power that sexuality can bring. Sex can be a wonderful, giving and goddess-like experience, and it can also be terrible and destructive. There's a level of consciousness required in it, and if you don't have that, it can lead to consequences you didn't intend.

Harb: From baby warrior to full-grown warrior

Harb, whom you'll recall moved from Malaysia to secure a successful journalism career in Australia, articulates her journey from baby warrior to full-grown warrior according to the three stages of life in the Indian tradition. I love this story because it is steeped in deep compassion for the baby warrior, fighting against injustice in a world skewed by prejudice.

In Indian traditions, they call the three stages of life the Three Dramas. The first one is the Brahmachari, which is about youth and learning. It's more hormonally turbulent by its nature.

Then, there is Grihastha, which is when you have your family or career, accumulate your wealth, and bring up the kids, or whatever that looks like for you.

The third drama is Vanaprastha. Vanam means forest in Sanskrit. It's the stage of the forest dweller, of spirituality, service and, hopefully, wisdom with that.

I can't remember exactly when it shifted for me, but it shifted into a deeper knowing and not having to fight so hard to speak from a place of wisdom.

I saw this statistic that 1 in 3 female staffers in Parliament are sexually harassed. You know, that's unbelievable. A journalistic study also showed that women write only 1 out of 3 opinion pieces. So, it's skewed. It's weighted towards the male voice. Gender is skewed even today!

I'm a member of that gender being discriminated against and of a race that's marginalised. I suppose, to some extent, I had to be the baby warrior as a young person. I understand that.

The baby warrior, for me, was having to fight for what I wanted. In a very warrior-like way, the relationship and breakup (from my first husband) were dramatic. And it wasn't from a place of wisdom; it was from a place of reaction that I couldn't live this kind of life anymore. I knew there was much more, and I was going to find it. I basically threw myself at a therapist's door. It turned out to be very, very good.

The baby warrior energy was useful in the sense that I left Malaysia as a 20-something to come and live in Australia, and I didn't think for once that I might not get a job or that it might be hard or what would happen if I didn't like it. I was just thinking, 'I'm going and leaving my life, all my friends I went to university with, all those I had been working with. I'm getting on a plane, and I'm going.'

I had written to both The Herald and The Age newspapers. A warm response had come from The Herald. I arrived in Melbourne and went for an interview and got the job. There was a sense of not worrying. I then progressed in the organisation and got promoted, getting more money and having more demanding and interesting roles. That was the reality for me – fighting for what I wanted. The baby warrior isn't just fighting and reacting. It's putting yourself out there, saying with confidence: I can do this. Yes, I can do that.

I'm not talking about those early days from a victim mentality but rather from a perspective where I was aware of the barriers and pushing through those. There is a fighter quality there. I knew that when it came to wielding my own power, I had to fight for it.

It probably started when I was even younger. I came from quite a conservative family. The Punjabi Sikhs are a very small but conspicuous percentage of the 15% of Indians in Malaysia, and they are very conservative. I had to fight to take a stand and even be allowed to go to a friend's birthday party. When I wanted to buy my first car, it was such a struggle for my family to allow me to do it and drive around in it because there was this fear of calamity. So, I had to assert, assert, assert, and I wasn't very gracious about it. It was full-on shouting, and I think I was trained to be a baby warrior by circumstances.

As I got older and got more of a sense of myself, I became more of a full-grown Karma warrior. I would speak up against inequity, injustice and racial discrimination, which really bothers me and gets me fired up. But I might navigate it in a different way, in a calmer way, and through an awareness that those things are still happening and that there's injustice and inequity.

When you come from a more solid position where you know yourself, there's a different reaction, a calmness. It's the difference between screaming and eloquently putting your point across.

For example, I was enraged and upset about what's happening in Australia, triggered by the George Floyd killing in America, which was so obvious and in-your-face undeniable racism. Killing someone on the street in such a brutal fashion was shocking. I knew I could help with my voice and be enraged. I wrote a piece for The Age newspaper about that, which was a more useful expression of strong energy and a wiser way of channelling it. It's like when you turn on the tap, and if you don't hold the hose properly, it goes flying everywhere. But when you hold the end of the hose, you can water the plant.

When you are a baby warrior, and you are fighting for justice, truth, inequality and change, you take on a Yang quality – which, in Chinese philosophy, is the active male element of the universe. And when I took on this Yang quality, I found it harder to soften into the family. I noticed that in relationships, too, it would be harder for me to lean into a man and to lean into receiving in a more feminine way.

I now find that with a more cultured, grown-up and mature warrior, I'm able to be articulate and passionate. There's a softness, to a large extent, when it comes from love. Even if it's rage, it's rage mixed with love and softness because you care enough to be passionate with love and softness. There's an ability to lean into a lover and to allow myself to be more feminine.

Another very important aspect of that is allowing myself to sink into the quietness of living. Because I'm sinking into the quietness of the Yin, which is the active female element of the universe, whatever action coming from that space moves into the Yang action in a deeper way. I call it feminine because it comes from this space of depth, and the action arises out of that.

For example, when George Floyd was killed with a policeman's knee to his neck, my rage was so intense that I poured it into a comment piece for The Age and The Sydney Morning Herald. It was titled 'A rage that is not in isolation' and was well-read. The response was very encouraging in terms of creating a better world for everyone. And when my son was racially discriminated by police because of the colour of his skin, I channelled the pain and rage into an articulate, strong letter to every relevant Minister and Shadow Minister at the state and federal level to draw attention to the problem of racism in our backyards.

Harb saw injustice in the world and, feeling the anger, acted from a place of love and compassion and considered all perspectives to find a solution that moves away from a win–lose situation and leans into a more collaborative, connected situation. This is the strength of feminine power.

Chapter 9

Growing Your Power
☆ ☆ ☆ ☆ ☆

Growing power and leadership requires desire, followed by action. Desire is the why; the mindset that says you're already powerful and deserve to grow your power. That belief system drives motivation to look for, and lean into, experiences that build self-efficacy and confidence.

Opportunities that lead to increased experiences of success increase confidence, and confidence leads to greater awareness and willingness to engage in further experiences that continue to build confidence – the perfect self-fulfilling prophecy ensues.

But what if motivation is more complex for women? From decades of social science[20], we know the structure of opportunity that first leads to those early experiences, which increase confidence and mastery, are often gendered.

Early on, socialisation processes shape women's aspirations and motivations, directing them to consider a limited set of occupational choices. This limited range

---

[20] J Palermo, Gender and Organisational Culture: Relationships between Women's Marginality and Career Success, LAP Lambert Academic Publishing, Berlin, 2010.

has an impact to diminish leadership expectations for women, as they recognise the constraints within the world of work. At the same time, the lack of opportunities and experiences, impacts motivation and limits leadership potential.

In addition to achievement, women face issues of balance, connectedness and interdependence. At any point, women may place primary emphasis on family and personal relationships and primary concern on career and personal achievements at work. So, as they try to strike some sort of balance between the two, they are likely to not only be concerned with their career but also on the welfare of others. At any point in time, women will place different degrees of emphasis on their actions and decisions based on these collective rather than individualistic considerations.

What enables women's growth in leadership and power are organisational cultures, where they can grow power in both realms. Instead, what we have, still in 2022, is a reality where women's earnings are penalised by their disproportionate responsibilities for work and domestic labour. When we study sub-units in organisations with less power, we find that they comprise groups of people with the lowest salaries and greater responsibilities for household work and domestic labour.[21] Unsurprisingly, these individuals are, in the majority, also women.

So, how do women grow power in their leadership when they are trying to successfully integrate both models – succeeding in a masculine and hierarchical model – whilst attempting to reject it? Rising to true feminine power is pursuing power in its relational, connected sense. Growing power for women, then, is about resolving this conflict.

Pauline: I want it all and it won't be perfect

More and more women are doing it and proving they can have the kids and the career. It's okay that you might be feeling that you are not doing everything well. It's okay to be imperfect. It's okay that you might be doing that one thing really well and some of these other things not so well. Or that you pull back a bit.

---

[21] K Cannings, 'An interdisciplinary approach to analyzing the managerial gender gap', Human Relations, vol 44, 1991, pp 679-698.

Don't feel that you've got to choose one aspect of your life over the other if that's doing yourself or your family a disservice, or feel that you're doing your employer or your team a disservice. You can create the life you want – be transparent, vulnerable and honest. I won't deny the fact that it can get tough, but it can absolutely work! It's just going to work for you in bits and pieces. You have to let go of expectations that it needs to be this or it needs to look like that all the time. It won't be perfect. It just won't be.

Another thing I would say to women aspiring for leadership is to jump into an opportunity even before you believe you can actually do it – fake it till you believe it.

So often, I interview women who feel the need to prove themselves, and they doubt themselves. I had someone whom I wanted to put into a C-level Executive role. She's in her early 30s. I've talked to her about it, and she said, 'I was going to talk to you about what's next, Pauline, but I felt like I needed to prove myself.'

She talked about all the ways she wasn't right for the role; she listed all her gaps. I had to remind her that even though she wasn't performing those tasks and demonstrating those skills now, what she had been doing was transferable to the leadership role.

Jo: Stay calm and take control

Jo was inspired in her early career by a female leader who knew how to command power in her own right and was so inspirational that it changed the trajectory of Jo's life.

I had every intention of joining the pharmaceutical industry as a scientist. I joined an agency as an active career-seeker in research and development, having travelled around the globe and ending up in London with that intention. I signed up with them, and as I was having conversations, this conversation about me changing careers and going into recruitment instead came up. The proposition was presented to me, and I took the plunge. And then the head of the recruitment company guided me along the way.

She was awesome. She had this innate ability to remain calm yet come across as professional and profound. She communicated effectively. Her motto was 'Take and maintain control of the situation. For every action, there is an effect.'

In other words, whatever you come across – whether you have to give a presentation at a networking event for the first time, or you're meeting a client and getting to know them, or you're talking to a candidate, and it's a new area for you – the question to ask is, how can you guide the conversation so that you're getting the best out of it for them and that they feel it's a mutual interaction?

Taking and maintaining control is not fumbling, not stumbling, not lacking confidence. It's just trusting yourself. In other words, irrespective of what other people are saying or how they're behaving, you remain grounded and unflappable.

Career-coaching helps women find their voice. It's about bringing out their self-confidence, which are themes that consistently come up. It's the question mark around 'Can I do this?'. Because they haven't visualised themselves in the next role, they feel like it's not possible to do it. They may think they need someone to validate their skills when, in fact, they need to self-validate. That's a common theme I see, even to date. With women, especially.

In 2020, there was a mixed bag of women and men needing coaching for their next step. As time progressed, in 2021, 75% are women seeking coaching. And now, in 2022, 90% are women saying, 'I need some support.' They're saying, 'I'm over the culture' or 'they're not going to allow remote as much as before, and I don't like the inflexibility. I don't necessarily want to go back into the office' or 'I want to step up' or 'The last couple of years has shown me that I have no career pathway'. These are themes that come up within life science and STEM careers.

As for me, I would like to elevate all women's voices as well as their allies' by sharing their personal experiences. Through doing that, I inspire others to speak, share, learn, teach and innovate. We need more of that. The more we see it, the more we feel like we can also contribute. Then, self-confidence starts to get built. If we see that more and more and feel that encouragement and support, we can keep that imposter syndrome, which is always there, at bay.

Chapter 10

Keep Your Power
☆ ☆ ☆ ☆ ☆

Power in an organisation is socially constructed and defined by the powerful. When viewed from an individualistic or masculine perspective, power is defined as an individual's real or perceived ability to influence others or have power over others. It equates power with who you are in comparison to others.

As we've seen from the stories in this book, women differ in their beliefs, values and attitudes towards power. Women may find some forms of power distasteful, particularly as it's expressed as power over others rather than power with or for others.

Power for others reflects a more feminine perspective. Women's concern for others and their more connected and communal orientations help them locate power within relationships. So, they're more inclined to distribute the benefits of power rather than be motivated to seek power in individualistic terms. This equates power with what you do **with** others rather than **against** others.

Myths do prevail in society, such as men are more interested in acquiring power than women, or men and women differ in their motivations to seek power. Society equates certain characteristics to powerful people when these characteristics are, in fact, the consequences of power. For example, we believe people become leaders because they are articulate, confident and socially competent – but those characteristics are consequences of being in leadership. Individuals experience success in power and leadership through achievement and performance, which builds a repertoire of psychological resources in their jobs until they are indeed more articulate, confident and socially competent. It's the nature of the self-fulfilling prophecy.

Research has found that women and men differ in their strategies to influence others. Direct strategies are used more by people with more power, while indirect strategies are used more by individuals with less power. Reward, coercion, legitimate information and expert power are more associated with masculinity, while helplessness, false information, nagging and sexuality are more likely to be associated with what I would call **passive** femininity.[22]

People with power typically choose power strategies associated with men or masculine power, while people with less power typically choose power strategies associated with women. While both men and women can use feminine power strategies, women tend to avoid masculine strategies.[23] Men may feel free to use a wider range of strategies to influence others. In contrast, there are detrimental effects for women who employ strategies that deviate from stereotypical gender role expectations. Women are evaluated more favourably when they use those weaker means of influencing others.

I often read articles on the ways women give away their power[24] that miss the reasons why women struggle with power in the first place. We have spent most of the pages in this book unravelling the factors that lead to this struggle. With that

---

[22] T Falbo & LA Peplau, 'Power strategies in intimate relationships'. Journal of Personality and Social Psychology, vol 38, 1980, pp 618-628.
T Falbo, MD Hazan & S Limmon, 'The costs of selecting power bases or messages associated with the opposite sex', Sex Roles, vol 8, 1982, pp 147-157.
[23] BR Ragins & E Sundstrom, 'Gender and power in organisations: A longitudinal perspective', Psychological Bulletin, vol 105, 1989, pp 51-88.
[24] B Marcus, 'The 9 Top Ways Women Give Away Power', Forbes, 2015, https://www.forbes.com/sites/bonniemarcus/2015/09/21/the-9-top-ways-women-give-away-power/?sh=738b65289260.

context in mind, it is still helpful to turn our attention to what women are doing or saying that minimises or dilutes their power.

Women often use minimising language, unnecessarily apologise, let others take credit, are hesitant to self-promote and don't prioritise using influence and leveraging relationships. Women often fail to secure allies and champions and care too much about being liked. They ask for permission and multitask, trying to do it all.

The stories here are not about addressing these tactical strategies. That would be like placing a bandage over an open wound. Instead, they are about how women maintain power on their own terms and how they have used communal forms of power to build resilience for themselves and others.

Angelique: Finding support in other women

Angelique finds herself on an executive team with the usual characters, but this time, with a female ally.

> *In this organisation, both I and the CFO are women. For the first time, I'm not the Lone Ranger on the executive team, but the dynamics of the organisation are different. On the Executive team there's the CEO and his mentor who's got skin in the game because he's got equity in the company, so he's got every interest to make this company succeed. Then, you've got foreign ownership, so you've got other stakeholders overseas. On top of that, we're buying our products from M, so you've got another huge stakeholder on the left.*
>
> *It was interesting these last couple of days. I've sat through two half-days of quarterly reviews with each dealership. It was the first time for me and the CFO because we're each other's buddies now. As you can imagine, watching the dynamic of the big brother telling the little brother what to do was fascinating. Throughout the meeting, the CFO and I chatted virtually about the dynamics in the group in real-time. We would write, 'Oh, did you hear this?' and 'Oh, this is interesting, right?' We were like two kids in high school.*

The CFO asked a question in this session. She said, 'You spoke about customer feedback, and the customer feedback is not good in Adelaide. Can you give us a little bit more insight as to what the feedback is about?'

One of the executive members replied, 'Oh, look. Trust me, we're very vocal with our folks over there. They know every piece of it. We don't need to get into it right now. Let's move on.' In front of 20 to 30 people, the CFO got shut down.

She asked a legitimate question. Were we brought along to this review just to sit and look pretty and say nothing and listen? That's pretty much what it was.

We giggled about it, but I reached out to her straight away and wrote in our chat, 'You got shut down. I think it was a valid question. It was perfectly plausible for you to ask that question, and I would have asked that myself', and she knows that.

I love Angelique's story because it demonstrates how women can support each other to 'read the room'. It's exhausting when you must read the room and the dynamics as well as participate in it. You're doing double the work as everybody else, but Angelique and the CFO are sharing that load.

Recall the parable of the elephant and mouse I mentioned in Chapter 1. How the mouse knew everything about the elephant – his mood, likes and dislikes and whether the elephant would react to certain temperature changes. The mouse knew everything about the elephant, but the elephant didn't even notice a mouse was in the room. That's what Angelique and her colleague are trying to navigate – the elephant. And it's a big frick'n elephant! But they are doing it together. They are doing what they can because it's not in their control to change the elephant.

Often, it takes a catalyst and time to disrupt a team. The two women are working around the elephant, so they don't get stomped on, then changing the environment when they can, when the elephant is asleep or distracted.

It's a way to support each other; it's much more fun, and we clicked straight away. The CFO was there slightly before me. When I started, she could see straight away that she could trust me, and I could trust her. So, it's a lovely relationship.

In hindsight, if I look back at my career, I was one-track-minded. I wanted to grow my career and move up the ranks. I was going to go for it, which was great. But if I had a little bit more patience early on, and if I knew then what I know now, I would have taken my time to learn the environment around me, how politics are played and how to use those internal networks better. I think I would have had a smoother road and would have been better off psychologically. So, my advice to my younger self would be: Yes, have career aspirations, but getting there in the fastest time can have adverse consequences.

Beulah: In the driver's seat

Beulah is an advocate for well-being and growth. She works towards this in her role as a Psychologist, a mother/stepmother, partner and singer. Her advocacy and self-compassion have brought wisdom to herself now that she is keen to share with others.

I can now see that I had a traumatic childhood, and when things go wrong at an early age, that can be more complicated. If you've been negatively impacted in some way, that sets you about 10 steps behind everybody else. It took a lot of work for me to deal with that. It's been a huge turnaround to now sit in the driver's seat of my life, although I'm still not comfortable.

When I think back to that little girl I used to be versus who I am now, taking into consideration all the things other people say about me and how they see me, I've been the last cab off the rank trying to work all this out. But it's coming together now, and that's the message I want to get out to others.

You can work through this, and you can own your power. We have an important place in the world as women.

My passion for the next stage of my life is helping people see their worth and value. I want to do meaningful work, which is why I'm thinking of opening my own private practice.

Harb, on being powerful together

Harb has and continues to mentor and inspire many women. She continues to support and advocate for women in the small and large interactions of her life, with wisdom and compassion that is authentic, thoughtful and impactful and a belief that we are powerful together.

I went to a women's retreat recently, where I became familiar with two young women who were both pregnant. One of the women was talking about a very traumatic experience. She was sitting next to me, so I put my arm around her. I felt motherly towards her, so I stroked her hair in a very motherly way. It seemed right at the moment to do that. When I kissed her on the head, she bursted into tears. I just held her.

Sisterhood is important, particularly in spaces that are contained and safe. It's an honour to support someone in their emotional upheavals and distress. It provides an opportunity to be powerful together. You also get that social support in other contexts, such as women's groups and sports clubs like women's football.

Traditionally, men don't have the opportunity to express their feelings. I look at my father and his generation and compare it to my son's. It's way more open now, with men being more emotionally expressive, but I also know of women who say their partner would never talk about their emotions or topics like love. It is easier for women to talk to each other about these things.

I started a women's circle during the COVID-19 pandemic. I had been part of a bigger women's circle with younger women, which was fabulous. I also wanted a women's circle that was more culturally diverse and reflective of the diversity in Australia. This current group has women from backgrounds including Chinese, Somalian, Italian and Australian French Aboriginal. Then, there's me – a Punjabi Sikh Malaysian Australian. That richness of tradition that comes together beyond the commonality of the human condition is very potent.

At the start of the lockdown, I had this desire to start the circle. So, I asked these women, and they all said yes. There are five of us, which is very manageable. It's confidential, a sacred space. When the five of us gather, there's spontaneity, there's fun, there's magic. And something else happens. When we share, there is no hierarchy. We all share from a place of being equal. No one mollycoddles or passes judgment; it's very, very supportive.

I've described it like the trapeze artists in the circus where they can fly, take risks and trust to hold each other's hands when flying. The circle is like the safety net underneath us where we can all talk about our dreams and adventures we want to embark on as well as our deep inner lives. We can talk about our fears and step through doorways we've never stepped through before. The circle has turned out to be far more than what I expected it to be.

We meet every month and never miss it. We made some agreements, but there aren't roles or rigid structures. There's mutual respect and understanding of confidentiality. The circle is a sacred space where we can be wholly ourselves and open. We bring whatever we want to and hold each other through the process. There's respect for each woman and compassion and communication, so it's a very tight-knit community. We are honouring each woman's journey with true compassion and open hearts. That energy has allowed us to be an amazing support for each other. When the five of us are together, there's this quality of grace, and something greater than ourselves comes through.

Cindy discovers women's circles

After two visits from cancer, Cindy is convinced that life's challenges show up to teach, reveal or promote change in our lives.

I completed circle teacher training last year, so I'm qualified to run women's circles. For me, women's circles are about creating a sacred space. Getting women together and creating an opportunity for deeper sharing has a place in the corporate world as well. This is our way forward as women, particularly connecting, collaborating, co-creating and sharing. It's only through connection and being seen that we really do heal.

Women have beautiful conversations when it's just women. I also love working with men; I love how they think and their way of being in the world. But I've chosen to work with women, just for now.

One of the things I talk about a lot, especially when speaking to women, is the Whisper-Tap-Slap. It's tapping into our body's wisdom because our body is continually communicating with us. Our bodies will wake us up to a change through symptoms and signs of distress. At first, we might get a little whisper, then we'll get a tap, and then we'll get a full-on slap, especially if we don't heed the call.

For example, my first diagnosis of breast cancer was a tap. The second was a full-on slap, which jolted me into taking a different approach to my priorities when going through that a second time.

I encourage women to take a pause and listen to what their body is saying. So many women just override their intuitive knowledge, like I did. They don't listen and then end up sick. So, slowing down is key, as is authentic expression, connection with self and connection with others.

A circle of encouraging women who connect with their femininity to lead in a feminine rather than masculine way would be meaningful work and impactful. Imagine what it would feel like to know you've got sisters who have your back.

Beulah: Creating women's circles

Beulah has come full circle from starting from a position of no power in her early years to a level of acceptance, wisdom and power as she becomes the powerful woman she knows she can be, with a little help from her friends.

We can see ourselves as works in progress, evolving and developing. As we go through each stage in our lives, we need different kinds of support. That's the effective way of dealing with what's happening in your life rather than avoiding it and feeling you must get everything done yourself because that may not always be possible.

I love my women's groups. When I created a women's circle, I reached out to my networks and explained it's about us holding space for each other. How we work is going to be determined by ourselves. I reached out to a fair few people; some were interested, and some drifted off or couldn't commit.

We take turns talking about what's happening for us. It can be anything, whether we're struggling with reflecting on things that have worked well or didn't work out so well. We take turns going around the circle, and we share resources. We also have a Facebook group, so we can share anything that pops up during the week.

Women's circles can be very different, depending on the people involved – that's the beauty of it. You can make it work for you based on your interests, your inclination and your style. I'll probably look to do more of those groups once I transition into my next level of independent practice.

Elissa: Breathing oxygen into our inner sexual power

Life stages impact the support we need. Elissa has an intuitive sense of this and how sexual power can be transformed as we mature as women.

It's important to note that sexual drive changes when we become menopausal. We're compelled as women to go within ourselves. That's the time we go with taking away that fire. Women resist this; they take hormone replacement treatments and try to stay sexy to hold on to that youthful fire energy. But as we mature, we're meant to go into that place within ourselves where there is a different type of fire energy. The only way we can access it is through stillness and softness and feel that it's there. Then, we can breathe oxygen into that and light it up.

I recently had a beautiful five-day silent retreat with these gorgeous women. Through meditations, the facilitator took us through waking up all the energy centres. It was so beautiful to experience that bowl waking up. You sense it through the softness together, not through friction. It's like being in the valley, not at the top of the mountain.

Slowly, we brought out all the energy in a gentle way and laid down in a foetal position to hold the energy for ourselves. I mean, we're aging, and so our tissues are breaking down. If we tap into that softness, that life force, we can put that energy back into our tissue. But if our focus is still external, it's depleting the energy. Young girls don't realise that what they're doing is really depleting.

Chapter 11

Let's Fix Gender Equality for Good
☆☆☆☆☆

Famous American philosopher Hannah Arendt reminds us that whilst we can perceive power as descriptive of certain characteristics, such as confidence or charisma, power resides in the relationships we keep and the network of people deciding to give or withhold power. In this way, power is relational.

I have highlighted that women's unique strengths and communal orientation to self make them exert the kind of relational power required to benefit all parties in each situation. However, they face masculine-biased systemic structures in our society and workplaces, so inevitably, power is defined as power over others.

It is our responsibility to work together with other women and marginalised people to break the bonds of misogyny through every small or large action within our control. Julia Gillard took an opportunity in 2012 to raise awareness of systematic sexism in the Australian Parliament during her role as Prime Minister in a speech opposing a motion to remove Peter Slipper, the then Speaker of the House of Representatives, after revelations of his sexual harassment of a staffer.

In reaction to the Opposition Leader, Tony Abbott, accusing her of sexism, Julia Gillard let him and the other Parliamentarians have it! In a now-famous speech[25], she responded to the Opposition Leader's answer to a journalist's question about women being under-represented in institutions of power in Australia:

> *I was very offended personally when the Leader of the Opposition, as Minister of Health, said, and I quote, 'Abortion is the easy way out.' I was very personally offended by those comments. You said that in March 2004, I suggest you check the records.*
>
> *I was also very offended on behalf of the women of Australia when in the course of this carbon pricing campaign, the Leader of the Opposition said 'What the housewives of Australia need to understand as they do the ironing...' Thank you for that painting of women's roles in modern Australia.*
>
> *And then of course, I was offended too by the sexism, by the misogyny of the Leader of the Opposition catcalling across this table at me as I sit here as Prime Minister, 'If the Prime Minister wants to, politically speaking, make an honest woman of herself...', something that would never have been said to any man sitting in this chair. I was offended when the Leader of the Opposition went outside in the front of Parliament and stood next to a sign that said 'Ditch the witch.'*
>
> *I was offended when the Leader of the Opposition stood next to a sign that described me as a man's bitch. I was offended by those things. Misogyny, sexism, every day from this Leader of the Opposition. Every day in every way, across the time the Leader of the Opposition has sat in that chair, and I've sat in this chair, that is all we have heard from him.'*

Julia Gillard's speech, coined The 'Misogyny Speech', resonated with women globally. It revealed the chasm between Tony Abbott's views and half of the population. How can leaders be so out of touch? We can blame the leadership paradox here.

---

[25] J Gillard, The Misogyny Speech, speech transcript, Julia Gillard, 2012, https://www.juliagillard.com.au/the-misogyny-speech/.

Studies on leadership and power reveal a paradox – skills that help someone obtain power, like empathy and perspective-taking, deteriorate once people are in power. Remember that attention flows up, not down. So, leaders can lose touch with the people who gave them power in the first place. Once people assume positions of power, they act more selfishly, impulsively and aggressively and find it difficult to see the world from others' points of view.

In organisational research surveys, we see that the rudest behaviours, such as shouting, swearing and humiliating others, are more likely to come from people in positions of power.[26]

The challenge for us, then, is to focus on both individual leaders and the environment we aspire to in the future workplace. This requires continued vigilance and collective effort. I'm sorry, Gen Z, we are not there yet!

Pauline: One benefits, we all benefit

When I had my daughter, I didn't take maternity leave. Back then, there was no unpaid maternity leave, and the business was struggling with the idea of having to replace me because I was in distribution. So, I said, 'Look, don't replace me. I won't take leave, and I'll make it work.'

So far, I had an easy baby, so I was sure I could make this thing work. I worked from home and had team meetings in the house. I had the flexibility, and I went into the office when I needed to. I was breastfeeding in meetings, putting my milk in the staff room fridge. I had all the flexibility we have now but didn't back then.

One day, the CEO called me to the office. He said, 'You're causing a real stir with all this flexibility. We might have to pull back or do something about it.'

---

[26] D Keltner, 'The Power Paradox', Greater Good Magazine, 2007, https://greatergood.berkeley.edu/article/item/power_paradox#:~:text=The%20skills%20most%20important%20to%20obtaining%20power%20and,the%20way%20we%20see%20ourselves%20and%20treat%20others.

I asked, 'Am I doing my job?'

'Yes,' he replied. 'You're doing a great job, and it's like you haven't left.'

I asked, 'Well, who's complaining? Is it the bloody guys?'

'No,' he replied. 'It's actually other women. It's the other women in the organisation that have a real issue with your flexibility.'

I investigated and found out who these women were. They weren't leaders or managers; they were at a junior level. So, it was an interesting case of women pulling other women down.

I spoke to one of the women who was an influencer and said, 'I need your help here. This will never change for women who want to have families if we don't show them what is possible. As women, we want to do it all, and I reckon we can do it all. You want to stop this? Let me pave the way.'

'You're only able to get this sort of flexibility because you're in management,' she said, 'and I never will.'

'How do you know that?' I asked. 'You've got no idea like I had no idea I'd get this flexibility, so don't stop it. Please wait; let's just support me for now, so we can make a change for others later.'

It was a defining moment. She agreed and then quietened down the noise. That experience paved the way for women wanting more flexibility in the organisation then. It ended up with other women getting flexible working hours, and the women who complained did get what they asked for.

This is an interesting story because you can think about enhancing power at the individual level as enhancing power for all. For me, it was about the women embracing that power and supporting the sisterhood, those paving the way. She might benefit first, but then we will all benefit.

Change in power dynamics requires people in power to let go of power. That's why this kind of change is often difficult. People in power need to accept that the systems that have advantaged them to achieve their current positions have been biased towards other groups and, therefore, need to be changed.

Having quotas for women in leadership teams and on company boards is a strategy to address such an imbalance. It acknowledges that the quotas mitigate the effects of biases in the selection and promotion of women.

A common myth is that gender equality strategies dilute a merit-based approach to selection. However, this isn't the case. The playing field is unfair to start with and overlooks equally competent and sometimes more competent women just because of their gender. To leave the status quo is to disserve a merit-based system because the best candidates are not even considered. So, how do you persuade people to let go of power? Well, that's another book. That's the next book.

Harb, on convincing 'them' to let go of power

I don't think we will achieve equality if we continue doing things the same way. The solution lies in creating environments that acknowledge how we feel and building connections through more communal environments. You have to convince people to let go of a certain type of power. We need to do things differently. So, the shortcut might be to create a more communal environment. Then, all that gets worked out in the mix. You don't have to sequentially work through it.

I agree with Harb – we need to do things differently. According to the Women Economic Forum's Global Gender Gap Report[27], it will take 135.6 years (global average) before we achieve gender equality in four key dimensions (Economic Participation and Opportunity, Educational Attainment, Health and Survival, and Political Empowerment). Let's not wait that long!

---

[27] Global Gender Gap Report 2021, World Economic Forum, Switzerland, 2021, https://www.weforum.org/reports/global-gender-gap-report-2021.

Dina: Question everything

Question everything. There's so much stuff I just accepted as part of the role expectations of being a woman. It dawned on me quite a few years into my career. I realised that whenever we would have something like a morning tea in the office, it would always be the women in the kitchen, setting it all up and cleaning up afterwards. I never stopped to question that something didn't seem quite right here. I took it as: This is just what we do, and this is just how things are.

There's a great quote that I read once, and it stayed with me, 'Once you see sexism, you can never unsee it.' And it's so true! I see it everywhere all the time now, just screaming at me.

In hindsight, I probably would have liked it if I had started to question things a lot earlier. It's something that comes with confidence and experience. Early in your career, you probably don't have the confidence to do that, but then you start to question, 'Why am I being asked to do this?' or 'Is this my job?' or 'Does this feel right?' If you question everything, you're also questioning your own bias.

I think about it in reference to other women. In the last couple of years, I have made this conscious effort to connect with all the women in my network, private and professional, and find ways to lift them up. I spent so much of my youth feeling I had to compete with other women and see them as a threat. I think we've kind of got talked into that dynamic. It really serves the patriarchy quite well – or it has served the patriarchy quite well.

Now I've woken up to it, and I'm making this conscious effort not to be the sort of person who would have had a lot of judgment around certain professions like sex workers. I would have absolutely held judgment towards that population before.

It's amazing once you open your mind and start questioning some of these thought processes. I'm their biggest advocate now. I'm the biggest advocate for doing whatever you do, whatever makes you happy, where you find passion and fulfilment, and all those sorts of things.

For me, equality is a women's issue. To be perfectly honest, I don't care what men do with their lives. That sounds so wrong, as I have a son I absolutely adore. I just feel that it is the systemic things we've talked about. If we are to have any chance of addressing those systemic challenges, then we have to find ways to lift up minority groups. And yes, it's women that are in the minority. Obviously, it's the gender-diverse, transgender and First Nations people as well who face inequalities.

We must actively work to remove those barriers. Questioning everything is a good starting point. I don't think I have any more valuable advice than that at this stage in my career, but maybe check in 10 years from now.

Now I see women as a gift to the world because that's what they are. They have so much to offer in so many ways, and it's beautiful. So, I like to explore that and learn about women's experiences because we don't get to talk enough about this. It's all a big taboo.

Lucia's plea: Show up and share stories

Lucia is aware of the mentors in her life and their impact.

I wish women leaders would be more active and show up more for younger, less experienced women. We want to see you. We want to see what you did. We want to see what you stand for. We want to see the pain you went through. Young women are always fighting until they reach the point where they come into their own. So, share your story, be heard, be you, and just be out there.

Mentoring, as well, is a great symbiotic way where both women help each other. Together we can shift the barriers, so many women are facing.

Jo, on collective ambition and choosing wisely

My cheat codes to getting ahead are to get a mentor, a coach, a support network and peers who will help you succeed, lift you up and constantly want to raise standards. If your network is no longer serving you, don't be afraid to move forward and let it go. That's one of the key learnings. Just because a person has been a mentor of yours for a period, it doesn't mean they're always going to be. You're growing and evolving, moving ahead and changing; some people will be okay with that. Other people might not necessarily be, and that's nothing against you. Everyone has their own journey.

I also think that ambition can be collective, which we could strive for rather than thinking about our careers as a solo journey. When you think about your outcome, how can you bring people on the journey with you?

You can still have your ambition and achieve greatness, but you can also take people on that journey with you as opposed to fighting them to get to the top. Because when you get there, it's lonely. If you had to fight your way up, you'd be there on your own instead of achieving collective success. Ultimately, that's where the fulfilment in leadership really comes from.

I want to encourage people who think they need to step over others just to get ahead, to think differently about it. Even though you may feel like that's fine now, it will catch up with you. You will come to a point where it doesn't feel right; it doesn't feel good. So why not do the right thing, and offer support if you see someone needing it to get ahead? It's more values-driven, graceful and ultimately more fun that way.

Having worked in several different businesses, especially over the last seven years where I've been consulting across various sectors, I have discovered that the culture of the business does come from leadership and trickles down. I have seen things that have been horrible, and I've also seen things that have been amazing. When faced with the former, you have a choice whether to stay and be subjected to that or err on the side of what will empower you to be a better version of yourself.

In the same business, you can have inspirational leaders who support and empower, and others who want to take away your power to feel bigger and better than you because of their own insecurities. I've seen all behaviours in businesses, like people getting ahead and not caring about who they step on to do so. They're the ones to avoid completely.

Empowering, supportive leaders are more fruitful for the business and individuals. A ripple effect can be created by having a positive leader. It permits the next person to pass that on, which is what you want.

Unfortunately, not every business is perfect. If you look at any business, they have different departments with different styles of engagement and people from different walks of life and different life experiences. That's why you've got to empower yourself to make decisions for yourself when it comes to your career.

If it doesn't feel right, then quickly decide what you will do.

Olivia, on success being meaningful

Olivia is very clear about creating a career aligned with her collective values.

When I reach the heights of my career, I'd like to feel that I've had a meaningful career and reached my potential without being held back. I think that's what it would feel like to be at a high level, that I have contributed meaningfully. I don't want to look back with regrets.

Meaning comes from delivering good work, which has positively impacted others and has supported them in some way. I find it so meaningful when I can do coaching or deliver facilitation around developing action plans off the back of employee feedback surveys. I find it meaningful when someone comes up to me and says, 'Oh, I'm feeling so much better about the future now.' Being able to address the things that are impactful to people's experience of work and improve them is ideal.

Melanie: Always wear your white coat

Melanie received advice early in her career to maintain her uniqueness above all else.

Very early in my career, I had one manager who gave me great advice. I was walking through the office, and I had a white coat on. He looked up and saw me amongst everyone else dressed in black. We sat down, and he said, 'Melanie, always wear your white coat. Always be you and never try to be someone else.'

He knew where my career was heading and what I was doing at that point.

Recently, I contacted him on LinkedIn about an issue. He wrote, 'Melanie, you don't need my advice anymore. You are now the inspiration. You are the one that will bring women on the journey and give them a positive experience and support them to achieve incredible things. So, it's your turn now.'

Always wear your white coat; always be yourself. He was right. There'll be people who don't accept that, and now I know. If that's the case, don't hang out with those people. I don't work for those people; I find something different. But one thing I committed to doing was always to wear my white coat.

Ilona: Be comfortable with who you are

For Ilona, being her unique self was always the only choice despite pressures to conform to masculine templates of leadership and power.

Often, we're told as women to just be ourselves, right? But being comfortable with who you are is easier said than done. So many times, the women I've dealt with at the most senior levels, for whatever reason, felt less feminine than even the blokes. Are they being themselves or being the archetype of the leader, which society deems male?

When I was at Medibank, an external consultant who did a lot of work on people issues within the company said to me, 'You're one of the few people in a senior leadership role who still presents feminine, you haven't lost any of it.'

I don't think I've ever adjusted to being more blokey or something other than myself. I can be as feminine as anyone in my own way.

If we can encourage women to just be who they are and who they are comfortable being, and have other people accept that, then that's femininity, isn't it? Because you're going to get a whole range of people. I was a bit of a tomboy, so I could mix it with the blokes and have those conversations. I quite enjoyed it. But not everyone does, and that's okay. You just need to feel confident in who you are and what you bring.

Rachel, on connecting to a higher power

Rachel shares a secret with us about her inner knowing about the power of connection.

I came to an amazing realisation that God is actually a higher power. The higher power is your connection to yourself, so it does give you comfort to know that there is a higher power and a higher source – and it actually is yourself.

Having that realisation is pretty mind-changing. I don't really tell many people this because they'll think I'm a bit weird. But, knowing that is a superpower.

I know how to connect with the higher source through energy and chakra work, and I am practising to improve my connection with my intuition. I think this is why people need to slow down. That's the only time we can be truly in touch with our superpower – when that intuitive voice does come through, and you can receive messages from the higher source. Essentially, this is why we are taught to pray to God – to receive the messages in how to live our life.

Harb's wise words: Nurture young men

Harb feels optimistic when she looks to the next generation, especially the boys, who need to be made aware of their privilege.

I have faith in the next generation. I hear conversations from my son about appreciating the privilege of going to a good school and knowing that not everyone can have that. Recently, he went for a long drive with a classmate, and when he came back, I asked, 'Oh, what did you guys do during that long drive?'

'We were just talking about how we can be better people', he replied. 'We were talking about our faults that hold us back from being amazing and better people.'

I thought, Wow, this is the next generation!

There is also something in nurturing young men to be authentic, express themselves, and be curious about their real voices. Often, we're not that curious about the real voices of boys. Young girls, especially little girls, talk, talk, talk – that's the influence of socialisation. Young boys aren't encouraged to talk and show emotion. They're encouraged to be big boys and that kind of thing. That still happens.

We can hopefully make a small difference, and it must work with boys and girls – girls taking more space, and boys getting more in touch with their emotions and feelings and knowing their privilege.

Gwen: Why is it not okay?

We need more men to be curious about their impact on inclusion. We need to be compassionate with ourselves and others as we work through these impacts, and learn to do it better. We don't all have the answers, and we don't want to shut down the dialogue about sexual harassment and sexism. So instead, let's talk about it, ask questions and be curious and a little brave.

Gwen's experience with one of her male colleagues is a testimony to how we can stay connected to this dialogue in a real way.

There were four of us in a meeting: my male boss, a male Junior Manager and a female Senior Manager. The female Senior Manager and I worked on a lot of our women's initiatives together and had talked about how we make an impact in our working environment. My boss asked the Manager to do something he didn't want to do because the client was quite challenging.

My boss said to him, 'Just grow some balls!'

At this stage, I was still very much a people pleaser. I tended to let a lot of these things wash over me and didn't react fast enough. My friend, however, reacted quickly to these things. She called out our boss.

He asked, 'What did I do? What did I do?'

She glared at him and said, 'That is not okay. It's not appropriate!'

My boss stood up and walked off, still perplexed as to why she was offended.

The male Manager then turned to us and asked, 'Why is it not okay? What happened? Why is that wrong?'

That was the first time I saw a man enquiring about something like this rather than brushing it off. He went on to say, 'I hear this. We say this a lot amongst us guys. Nobody ever bats an eyelid, so why is this not okay?'

That was the first time I sat down and had this kind of conversation. We talked it through. That was the first time I saw a man pause and lean into it.

Tina, on evolving as a human being

Tina leaves us with wise words about *being* rather than *planning to be*.

Don't try and have everything mapped out and put expectations on yourself because you will only limit yourself. Instead, stay inquisitive, lean into situations even when it's scary, and be surprised by what you learn and where it takes you. Evolve as a human. I came to realise that much later in my life.

When you place expectations on your own self, you limit your very being. It puts you in that fixed box. By just leaning in, you could be so much more than you ever dreamed.

End Remarks

☆ ☆ ☆ ☆ ☆

When you see, you cannot unsee. I hope you have gained a new way of thinking about your relationship with power that aligns more closely with the full-grown feminine warrior within you – that powerful woman you know.

Be bold. Feel beautiful. Lead.

Acknowledgements

☆ ☆ ☆ ☆ ☆

Many women contributed to this book and shared their stories and viewpoints with bravery and trust. I thank them for their time and generosity. This book would not be possible without their beautiful voices.

Whilst all the women I interviewed have informed the thinking of this book, I want to thank those women who graciously allowed me to include their stories in its pages. They are:

Rebecca Aichholzer is a Salesforce MVP, Product Owner and proud Woman in Technology. As well as being Head of Business Systems Success at QIC Real Estate, she is also a powerlifter and strongwoman, having represented Australia twice in international competitions.

Melanie (not her real name) has had an extensive career in IT Program Management and has successfully delivered millions of dollars in value for her clients. She has led both business- and IT-related projects and programs of work in transitions, transformations, organisational change, strategy and education both in Australia and internationally.

Ilona Charles is the CEO and Co-Founder of Shilo People. She is an experienced Executive and Chief People Officer with more than 25 years of experience in human resources, transformation and change.

Tina Custer is a Business Improvement Manager with over 10 years of experience working with companies undergoing transformation towards improved customer experience and employee engagement. She combines project management, process improvement skills and facilitation experience with a strong empathic approach to people, which has led to the successful delivery of many cross-functional projects in various engineering companies.

Olivia Dineen is Psychologist specialising in organisations with a demonstrated history of working in professional consulting, private sector and government agencies. She is skilled in organisational development, psychometric assessment, talent management, leadership development, culture assessment, employee engagement and health and well-being.

Gwen Faure has spent her career as a consultant, leading transformation programs for global clients in financial services. She is passionate about women's empowerment and believes everyone has the right to shine in their own way.

Justine Figo LLB (Hons) FCPHR has held multiple senior HR leadership roles and is the author of Connect Better Faster and On the Same Page: 5 Conversations Leading for Top Team Cultures. In addition, she is the founder of a flourishing HR Executive Community and is a sought-after coach.

Harb Gill is an award-winning editor and writer who has worked on major daily newspapers and top magazines in Australia and overseas. Her experience includes work for The Age, Herald Sun, Monash University, The Saturday Paper and The New Straits Times.

Sue Hurly is an Organisation Design and Change Consultant with a Human Resources background and considerable experience working with Senior Management teams and boards across multiple industries and sectors. In her personal life, Sue has raised a 23-year-old daughter and attempts a regular practice of yoga, photography and walking in nature in her free time.

Dr Beulah Joseph is a Well-being Advocate, supervisor, educator and Organisational Psychologist. Her background in organisational psychology has given her a unique insight into human behaviour and the modern workplace and has

ACKNOWLEDGEMENTS

informed her work with organisations to enhance both business and individual employee outcomes.

Nicole Ma's award-winning projects include: the documentaries Dances of Ecstasy, Kurtal Snake Spirit and Be Happy Be Strong; the inaugural multimedia exhibitions for the centenary opening of the National Museum of Australia; and the blockbuster exhibition Yiwarra Kuju, featuring the history of the Canning Stock Route. Putuparri and the Rainmakers is a feature-length documentary that had its world premiere at the Melbourne International Film Festival, followed by an international premiere at the Hot Docs Film Festival. It has been nominated for many awards and won Best Film at the 2015 CinefestOz Film Festival.

Jo McCatty is a recent Head of People & Culture, career strategist, podcast host and advocate for getting more women into STEM and leadership roles. She is the Founder of Protoscience, which offers career coaching as a service through workshops, one-to-one coaching, and programs for tech, biotech, health tech, medtech and CRO sectors.

Rachel Saliba is a mother of three children, an entrepreneur, life coach, author, facilitator and speaker who is passionate about inspiring people, especially children and the adults who surround them, to reach their full potential in life. Rachel has worked extensively in education, delivering professional learning and coaching related to life skills and parent engagement. She has recently published her book to support parents as they guide and support their children's learning journey.

Lina Palermo is 78 years old, an Italian immigrant, mother, grandmother to three, ex-entrepreneur, socialite in the Melbourne Italian community and committee member of the Ibleo Italian Social Club. She is also my mother, friend and role model. She loves dancing and has a contagious laugh. On any given week, she is on the phone with hundreds of people, organising attendees for the Ibleo Club events and inspiring others in her community to keep dancing.

Pauline (not her real name) is a CEO and Managing Director. She is an experienced and charismatic leader with extensive expertise in her industry. Pauline is also a very proud mother of two young adults who still reside at home with her. She has a deep understanding of people and culture within business and is one of the best leaders I have witnessed, as she combines true feminine power in her authentic and compassionate leadership style.

Cindy Scott is the Founder of EvolvingWomen.co, author, podcaster, speaker and producer of cancer gifts and programs for women's resilience and well-being.

Dina Ward is an Organisational Psychologist, Talent Strategist and Diversity & Inclusion Manager. With more than 12 years of industry experience across public, private and not-for-profit sectors, she has successfully led solutions in talent acquisition, talent development, diversity and inclusion, culture change and transformation, organisational design and capability development.

Lucia Zelesco has been in business for the last 10 years, helping her clients all around the world grow with smart marketing. She has been a member of two boards and featured in national media.

Elissa (pseudonym) has held senior positions in the retail industry and has been a successful business owner. She now works in independent practice as a counsellor.

About The Author

☆ ☆ ☆ ☆ ☆

Dr Josephine Palermo has advocated for women and gender equality all her adult life. With a PhD in Organisational Psychology and numerous publications in coaching and leadership development, psychology of gender and organisational development, she is a sought-after speaker, leadership and team coach and mentor.

Josephine brings a deep understanding of gender and organisational dynamics to her philosophy of communal leadership. With experiences as an academic, Senior Leader in corporations, Organisational Consultant, business owner and community leader, she applies her knowledge of psychology and gender to practical strategies for bridging the gender gap in leadership.

Currently, she is fulfilling a lifelong ambition of entrepreneurship as Director of several businesses, including Geared for Growth Consulting, Higher Spaces Coworking and Melbourne Bellydance. Josephine challenges us to think differently about the meaning of work in our lives so that we can bring our whole selves to work. In 2020, she launched a podcast called Gears, Action, Growth (www.playpodca.st/gearsactiongrowth), where she discusses topics related to business culture and teams with special guests.

JOIN OUR FACEBOOK GROUP

https://www.facebook.com/groups/risingtofemininepower/

CREATE A WOMEN'S CIRCLE

www.risingtofemininepower.com

CONTACT JOSEPHINE

Website - www.gearedforgrowth.biz/contact

Via social media - www.linktr.ee/gearedforgrowth

Notes
☆☆☆☆☆

www.ingramcontent.com/pod-product-compliance
Lightning Source LLC
Chambersburg PA
CBHW051331110526
44590CB00032B/4478